WINNING FORMS™
EXCEL FOR WINDOWS

Jim Kinlan,
Jack McGrath &
Scott Tucker

RANDOM HOUSE
ELECTRONIC PUBLISHING

New York

Manufactured in the United States of America

98765432 24689753 23456789

First Edition

ISBN: 0-679-74292-1

New York   Toronto   London   Sydney   Auckland

Acknowledgments

Getting a book—and diskette—out the door is not a simple process. Any name on the cover is really the point person for a team of people. In this case, we benefitted immensely from the willing and cheerful ideas and energy of Melanie Meeker Jones and Doreen Menard. Early in the process, Gene Timony and Peter Marx played pivotal roles in testing the base products.

Among our friends at Random House, we'll sorely miss Julie O'Leary, soon to be PhD-ed. She not only has kept track, but kept everything on track as well. Thanks to Mia McCroskey and our favorite visionary and publisher, Michael Mellin.

This book is dedicated to Carol, Marcia, and Margaret. One of these days, we'll resurface—for dinner at Biba.

CONTENTS

INTRODUCTION

Welcome to *Winning Forms for Microsoft Excel*. You're just a few minutes away from harnessing Excel and your printer to produce professionally designed forms, calendars, and personal planning tools.

Winning Forms for Microsoft Excel is designed to:

- **Improve Your Image.** Whether you are a small business owner or work in or manage a corporate department, *Winning Forms for Microsoft Excel* will help you to present a polished, professional image in minutes. Appearance isn't everything, but such things as your invoices, cash receipts, and FAX covers can make the difference between whether customers and suppliers pay attention or yawn in your business presence.

- **Save Time.** The time you spend building, shipping, or selling your product is time spent earning. When you have to stop and design a Fax or memo form, or come up with a purchase order form, you are not spending your time well. You may think of that time as a learning cost, but few small business owners or corporate managers can afford the luxury of learning to do things they will do only once. Buying a specialized forms design program is not a solution, because you have to spend the time to learn the program. *Winning Forms for Microsoft Excel* works with software you already own and know how to use. And because every form in *Winning Forms for Microsoft Excel* can be printed on plain paper, you can print them at your convenience—not the printer's.

- **Save Money.** You can print one or one hundred copies of a form, so you won't tie up money stockpiling forms you don't need. Some stationery companies and suppliers now stock perforated paper that you can use in a laser printer, so that the recipient of your form can separate it and return part of it to you. And if you need multipart forms, you can also buy collated, colored paper for laser printers. What's more, *Winning Forms for Microsoft Excel* can be customized in-house, so you'll also save money and time on design.

What You Need To Use This Book

To use this book and the files contained on the disk, you must have an IBM or IBM-compatible computer with enough RAM (Random Access Memory) to run Excel, and a floppy disk drive that can read

720K disks. You should also have a VGA, EGA, high resolution CGA, or Hercules graphics adapter and monitor.

You must also have Microsoft Excel Version 4.0.

Although you can install *Winning Forms for Microsoft Excel* on a high-density floppy, we recommend using your hard disk.

You can use some of the forms in this book without a printer, but not all of them. You should have at least a 24-pin dot matrix printer. If you own an ink-jet printer, such as a Hewlett-Packard DeskJet, you will be able to use any of the forms on the disk. The forms are most effective when printed on a laser printer, such as the Hewlett-Packard LaserJet series.

Conventions

In general, if you are familiar with the your Windows documentation or the Excel *User's Guide*, you will understand all of the instructions in this book. A few of the more important conventions, however, are worth repeating.

All instructions use the term choose, as in Choose File Open. Choose File Open means to point with the mouse to File in the menu bar at the top of the screen, click the left mouse button, then point to Open and click the left mouse button again. (Assuming that you have not switched mouse buttons.) That will open the File Open dialog box. When the dialog box appears, you will be instructed to click one or more of the various buttons or text boxes.

If you are not using a mouse, press the [Alt] key whenever an instruction begins with choose, then press the arrow keys ([↑], [↓], [→] or [←]) to choose the appropriate menu and submenus, pressing [←Enter] when you have navigated to the correct choice. Once you have reached the dialog box, navigate it with the Tab key ([Tab ⇥]). Choose File Open means that you should press the [Alt] key, point to the menu option File, press [←Enter], point to the Open option, and press [←Enter] a second time. Alternatively, you can type the first letters of each menu option. That is, typing [Alt] FO is the same as choosing File and then choosing Open.

When we instruct you to type something, we mean that you should type the characters exactly as they are shown. Whenever you are told to type something, we will include every character you must type:

C:\DIR ⏎Enter

How To Use This Book

This book is designed to be used as a reference. You will profit most from it if you use it as you use the manual that comes with any software. The heart of this book is the enclosed disk; the purpose of this text is to illustrate and explain the files on that disk.

As you can see by leafing through this book, each form on the disk is illustrated on a right-hand page. These examples contain fictional data to show you how to use the forms. The forms on the disk do not contain the data nor the company or individual names that you see in the illustrations. Virtually all of the forms on the disk can be printed as blank forms, to be filled in by hand or on a typewriter.

The text on the left-hand page describes how to use the form, how to enter data into it, how to print it, and how to adapt it. Occasionally, the left page will also contain a few notes about some of the formulas in the form. Most of the discussions of forms are keyed to the illustrations numerically. When you see a number in a bracket in a discussion it corresponds to a number, printed in grey, on the form on the facing page

Chapter 1 consists of a brief overview of the forms, and tells you how to install and use them. We recommend that you read all of Chapter 1; but if you do not, each section in the chapter contains all of the information you will need to deal with the topic that section covers.

CHAPTER
1

_____

USING WINNING FORMS
FOR MICROSOFT EXCEL

Winning Forms for Microsoft Excel consists of 112 files designed to help you control and manage your business and personal affairs. The goal of Winning Forms is to free you from the often onerous task of designing forms.

We are making a few assumptions about you. First, we assume that you already own and use Excel. And we assume that you do not have time to invest learning all there is to learn about Excel to turn out forms that are professional-looking and effective. Finally, we assume that you also do not want to spend time learning a program designed to design forms.

Overview

Winning Forms for Microsoft Excel consists of six categories:

The *Administrative* category contains calendars and time-planning forms, and such forms as appointment schedules, memos, and Faxes.

The *Finance* category includes a basic set of financial forms such as balance sheets and income statements, various credit forms, invoices, expense reports and budgets, and so forth.

The *Human Resources* category contains forms for hiring, training, and administering employee records.

The *Operations* category contains forms for inventory control and management, shipping, production, and purchasing.

Forms in the *Personal* category include a personal statement of net worth, investment management and goal-setting forms, and forms for calculating mortgages, life insurance, and college funding.

Finally, the *Sales and Marketing* category contains forms to help you track sales prospects, project sales, analyze a direct mail campaign, and so on.

It is unlikely that you will need or use every form in the Winning Forms package, but most small business owners and individuals will probably find a number of forms to use daily or weekly. Even if you do not need every form in this package, the day will come when you need one—and only one—copy of a form. Look for it here first, because if you head for the business supply store, you will find that forms are like potato chips—you can't have just one.

Installing Winning Forms for Microsoft Excel

Winning Forms for Microsoft Excel is simple to install. To begin, insert the Winning Forms disk in drive A or B and make the drive you chose current. (We assume you will use drive A for this process. If not, substitute B for A in the instructions that follow.) If you are at the DOS prompt, and want to install *Winning Forms for Microsoft Excel*:

1. Type A: `←Enter`
2. Then type INSTALL `←Enter`

If you are already in Windows you can install *Winning Forms for Microsoft Excel* either:

1. By opening a DOS window and using the procedure described above; or

2. From the Program Manager, by choosing File Run and typing A:\INSTALL or B:\INSTALL and clicking OK: or

3. By opening the File Manager, double clicking on the drive containing the *Winning Forms for Excel* disk and double clicking INSTALL.EXE.

Whichever way you use to begin the installation of *Winning Forms for Excel*, when you begin installing *Winning Forms for Excel* your screen should look exactly like the one shown in Figure 1.1.

Figure 1.1 The *Winning Forms for Microsoft Excel* Installation screen.

If you need help at any time during installation, just press the Help key, F1 . Otherwise, just follow the instructions you see on the screen. Figure 1.2 shows a Winning Forms Help screen.

You may install all of the Winning Forms or only those in a particular category. To select a category of forms, highlight a category name, and press Spacebar . As shown in Figure 1.3, a check mark appears next to a selected category, and the description box beneath the category list shows how many forms there are in the category and how much hard disk space they require. When the install program begins, all six categories are selected. You may change the selections by pressing ⌈Spacebar⌋, or you may select all categories by pressing ⌈F10⌋. To install every category in Winning Forms you will need approximately 1.4 megabytes of hard disk space.

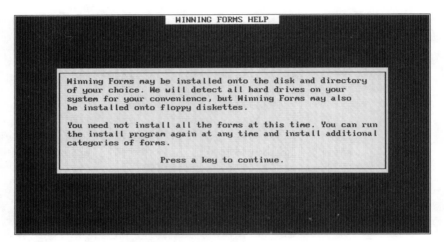

Figure 1.2 The Winning Forms Help screen.

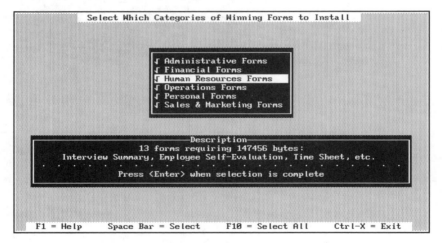

Figure 1.3 Selecting forms for installation.

When you have finished installing Winning Forms, you will see the screen shown in Figure 1.4. Before continuing, remove the disk from the drive and store it in a safe place.

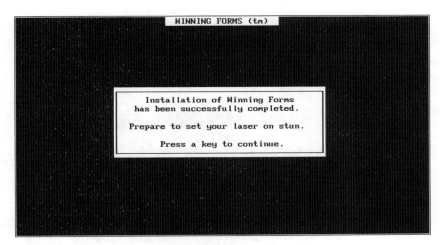

Figure 1.4 The Installation End screen.

Throughout the text that follows, we assume that you installed *Winning Forms for Excel* in a directory named C:\WF. If you chose another directory name, substitute the name you use at installation for \WF in the instructions that follow.

Retrieving a Winning Forms File

After you have installed the Winning Forms files, start Excel and set the file directory to C:\WF by choosing File Open (or typing Alt FO) and typing C:\WF\←Enter in the File name text box. Excel will display the Winning Form files in the directory, as shown in Figure 1.5.

If you wish to change to that directory permanently, you will have to edit your EXCEL4.INI file to contain the line OPEN=/PC:\WF. Each time you start an Excel session after that, you will be able to load a file just by choosing File Open.

Double click the file name or point to the file you wish to use, and Press ←Enter.

Every Winning Forms filename begins with a prefix that tells you to which category the form belongs. The categories and the filename prefixes are shown in the table below.

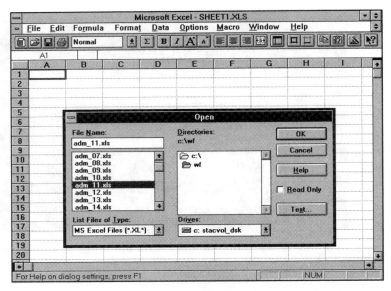

Figure 1.5 Opening a Winning Forms file in Excel.

So, if you want to retrieve a form for personal planning, you would place the pointer in the File name text box of the File Open dialog box, and type PER*.xl*⏎Enter. Then, only those files in the directory that begin with PER would be displayed.

Table 1.1 Form Category and Filename Prefix

Category	*Prefix*
Administration	ADM
Finance	FIN
Human Resources	HUM
Operations	OPR
Personal Finance and Planning	PER
Sales and Marketing	SAL

Go Home for Help

Each Winning Forms file contains two windows: A reference window and a form window. When you open a Winning Forms file for the first time, you will see its reference window, a screen of introductory information about the form. Figure 1.6 shows a typical reference window, which tells you about the form, how to enter data into it, and how to print it.

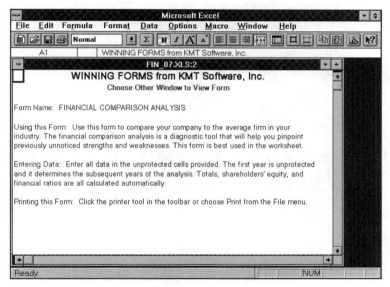

Figure 1.6 A typical reference screen.

In many Winning Forms files, most of the data needed for a form is entered into the body of the form itself, which you can access most easily in the form window. In a few cases, however, a file may contain data cells that are not a part of the form itself, but into which you may or must enter data. For example, every form that contains a calendar also contains cells where you enter the month or year to produce the calendar you need. Whenever you have to enter data that is not in the form itself, the reference window will specify the cell address or addresses that you must use. All such cells are located in row 19 of a form, which is part of the reference window.

Before you begin working with any form you have retrieved, take a moment to read the text in its reference window. Pay particular attention to the Entering Data section, since that is the part of the text that contains the instructions you will use most often.

To view and work with the form itself, you can either choose the other window in the file from the Window menu, press [Page Down], or press [F6]. (If pressing [F6] does not take you to the other window, choose Workspace from the Options menu, and select the Alternate Navigation Keys button near the bottom of the Workspace Options dialog box.) Every form in *Winning Forms for Excel* begins on row 21.

If you find that you must frequently change some data that is on row 19 when you are working with a given form, go to the reference window and use the [Page Down] or arrow keys to view the form, then scroll the screen so that you keep row 19 on the screen while viewing a portion of the form. Figure 1.7 shows a screen in which both the data entry row and a form are on screen at the same time.

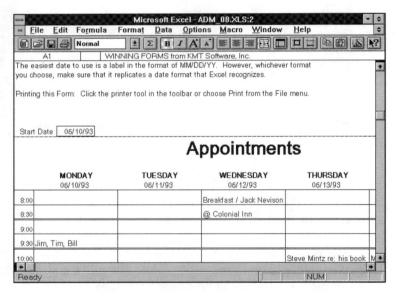

Figure 1.7 Part of the form and data entry section on the same screen.

Saving a Winning Forms File

After you have retrieved a Winning Forms file, and before you do anything else, you should save it using a new name. That way you protect the original version of the file, and do not have to repeat the installation procedure to recover the file. If anything goes wrong while you are working on the file (a loss of power, for example, or the accidental erasure of a critical part of the file), simply retrieve the original file and begin again.

For example, the Winning Forms file for the Monthly Calendar is in a file named ADM_02.XLS. After retrieving ADM_02.XLS, Choose File Save As (or type [Alt]FA) and save the file with the name, say, 92DEC (for December 1992). Then continue working. When you want to create a calendar for January 1993, you can retrieve either ADM_02 (the original file) and save it as 93JAN, or retrieve 92DEC, update it, and save it as 93JAN.

Entering Data in Winning Forms Files

All of the files in Winning Forms have been protected with the Options Protect Document Command. All of the cells into which you must enter data, however, are unprotected. Since the gridlines have been turned off in all forms, most unprotected cells are indicated on screen by light dotted lines. The exception to this rule is when an unprotected cell has a border. Figure 1.8 shows the Bank Reconciliation form, in which the values for the balances according to the statement and the checkbook are both unprotected. As you can see in the figure, the statement balance has a faint, dotted underline, indicating that the cell is unlocked, while the border beneath the checkbook balance suppresses the dotted line. Generally, you will have no problem about where to enter data, but if you are ever in doubt simply try entering data. If you try to enter data in a protected cell, Excel will beep and display a dialog box containing the message: Locked cells cannot be changed. In short, you need not worry about inadvertently damaging a Winning Forms file.

Entering Labels in Winning Forms

Most of the data you will enter into a file will be text data. In most cases, all you have to do is begin typing the text you want to enter. The various areas of the form that you will use for the text have already been formatted so that the text aligns correctly as shown in the illustrations. In some instances the form will contain an entry that describes the kind of entry you should make in a given location. Figure 1.9 shows a typical label entry prompt.

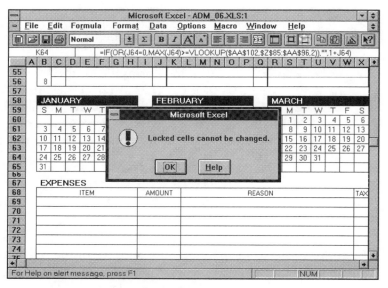

Figure 1.8 Unprotected cells in Excel.

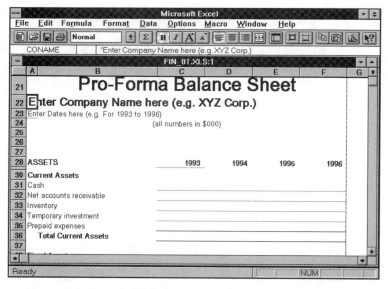

Figure 1.9 A typical label entry prompt.

Entering Dates in Winning Forms

Many Winning Forms files use the date arithmetic functions of Excel extensively. Although it helps to understand those functions, you do not have to master them to use dates effectively in Winning Forms. Every form that requires dates permits you to type the date directly into a single cell. So, if you were to enter *9/15/93* wherever you need to enter a date, the form you are using will understand that date automatically. In a few instances you must specify the day, month, and year, but dealing with dates in *Winning Forms for Microsoft Excel* never gets more complicated than that. In fact, if you want to use the current date, just type Ctrl ; ⏎Enter. That will enter the current date into the cell.

There is one requirement for using dates, however; you must enter the date in a format that Excel recognizes as a date. Those formats are:

- 01-Aug-93

- 01-Aug

- Aug-93

- 08/1/93 or 8/1/93

- 08/01

If you enter a date in any of those formats, the form will do the rest. In general, using the 8/1/93 format is your best strategy, since the space allocated in any form for dates will always accommodate that format.

Note that whenever you enter a month name, use only the first three letters of the name. (Capitalization does not matter. You can enter Sep, sep, sEP, etc.)

Two minor points are worth keeping in mind when you use such date formats in Excel. First, although Excel consistently precedes months or days with a zero when they are below ten, you do not have to do so.

Second, if you use the date formats that show only the month and day (15-Sep or 9/15), Excel will use the current year as the year. If you use the format that includes only the month and year (Sep-93), Excel will use the first of the month as the day. When Excel supplies the year or day, it uses the clock in your computer. If you have set the clock correctly, you will have no problems.

If none of the date formats that Excel offers fits your needs, you can create one of your own. For example, you may wish to add a date format that enables you to display dates in the format conventionally used in correspondence (May 7,1993). To do so:

1. Remove protection from the document (by choosing Options Unprotect Document or typing Alt OP), then;

2. Choose Format Number Date and select any format;

3. Click on (or Tab to) the Code text box, and;

4. Type mmmm d, yyyy. The Number Format dialog box should look like the one shown in Figure 1.10.

5. Press ↵Enter or click OK to return to the worksheet, and

6. Reprotect the worksheet by choosing Options Protect Document (or typing Alt OP) and clicking OK or pressing ↵Enter.

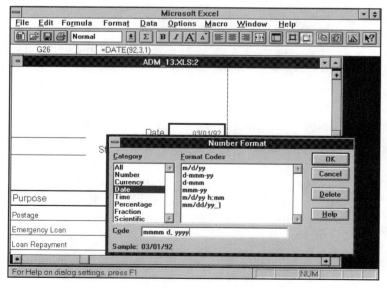

Figure 1.10 Creating a new date format.

Besides using entered dates most Winning Forms files will also accept standard Excel date functions, so you should be familiar with a few basic concepts about dates in Excel. The first point to understand is that as far as Excel is concerned, all dates are numbers between 1 and 65,380. If you enter any number in that range in Excel and apply a date format to it (choosing Format Number Date), you will have a working date. In Excel, the number 1 is defined as January 1, 1900, and the number 65,380 is defined as December 31, 2078. If you enter 34132 in Excel and then choose Format Number Date and select mm/dd/yy, Excel will display that number as the date 06/12/93. Similarly, if you enter and format 13701, Excel displays 7/05/37. To manipulate those numbers, Excel contains an assortment of built-in date functions that are already incorporated in the Winning Forms files for you.

Since many of the Winning Forms files can easily be linked to other Excel files, or be made part of a larger Excel template, we often suggest that you enter a date using the date function, DATE. If you are not familiar with the DATE function, here's a brief example of how to use it. Imagine you want to enter the date September 15, 1993. The DATE function requires three arguments, or items of data that you must supply: the year, the month, and the day, in that order. Thus, to produce the date you need, you would type =DATE (93,9,15)⏎Enter. Excel will display the value 34227. Then, choose Number from the Format menu, select Date in the Category list box, and click on mm/dd/yy in the Format codes list box. Alternatively, type Alt TN and tab to the list boxes, selecting Date and mm/dd/yy in each. Excel will display the number as 09/15/93.

Using the Winning Forms Calendars

Winning Forms for Excel contains a number of files that are either full calendars or that incorporate a calendar in some format. In most instances, you may enter dates in a number of ways. That is, you can usually enter months as numbers (e.g.,1–12) or as text (e.g., Jan, Feb, Mar). The monthly calendars (ADM_04 and ADM_05) and the Running Log (PER_06) will also accept the text *This, Last,* or *Next* for a month. If you enter any of those words, the file will use the current year and either the current month or the previous or next month. If you specify only the month in the Running Log, it will automatically use the current year. If you enter *This* and one of those forms does not display the true month and year, check your computer's clock.

The Quarterly Planner (ADM_03) will accept First, Second, Third, and Fourth (or FI, SE, TH, or FO) as well as a number (1–4) for the number of the quarter for which you wish to produce a form.

Formulas

A few Winning Forms files contain a large number of formulas. The yearly calendar, for example, contains almost 500. Most contain far fewer, and some contain none. In almost every file that contains formulas, however, the formulas have been written so that you can print the file without data and fill it in manually. A typical formula may look like this:

```
=IF(C5<>0,SUM(C1..C4),"").
```

That formula means that if there is a value in cell C5, the cell containing the formula will show the sum of the values in cells C1..C4; otherwise, it will show nothing. Occasionally, you may see similar, but far more complex formulas, but the goal is always the same— to prevent a calculation from appearing until there is data for it to work on.

The purpose of these formulas is to enable you to erase all data from a file and print the file as a blank that you can then fill in by hand. As an alternative, if you enter data, the results display and you can print a filled-in file.

On occasion, you may wish to edit a formula or replace a formula with a value. In such cases, you must choose Options Unprotect Document or type Alt OP. If you then proceed with care, you can change any cell you wish. Note that if you want to apply shading or change the color of text in a cell or cells, you must first unprotect the file.

Printing a File

Every form has been designed to print on one side of a single sheet of 8.5-by-11 inch paper. The necessary print area for each form has been defined, so it is not necessary for you to change it. In fact, we recommend that you avoid changing the print area unless there is absolutely no alternative. Printing a form then, is simply a matter of clicking the print tool in the Toolbar. Before printing, you may wish to choose File Print Preview, (or type [Alt]FV) to see how the form will look when it comes out of your printer. Figure 1.11 shows a Winning Form in the preview mode.

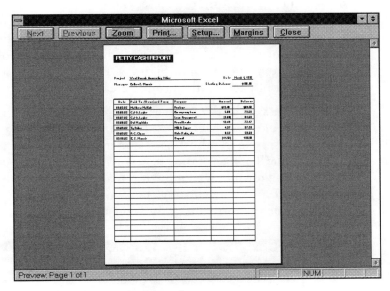

Figure 1.11 Previewing a form.

Customizing and Adapting a Winning Forms File

Although each form has been carefully formatted and professionally designed to make it easy for you to use and to help you present a professional image, you may wish to change the appearance of some forms. In this section we will show you some of the opportunities—and pitfalls—involved in changing a form. We'll also share a few tips about using the spreadsheet publishing capabilities of Excel.

Changing Fonts

Throughout all the Winning Forms files, we have used relatively few fonts (typefaces). We have used only the Arial font and only in four or five sizes.

Be careful if you replace any font in a form with one that is larger or smaller, but particularly if you use a larger font. In many instances, you may change the page break in a form by using a larger font. For example, the title of most forms is formatted to print either in 18 or 24 point Arial bold. If you decide to replace a title in 24 point Arial with one that is in 36 point Roman, you might force one or two lines of the form onto a second page. You should check your page breaks periodically by previewing the form. To do so, choose File Print Preview or type Alt FV. When in preview mode, check the lower left corner of the screen to see if the form consists of more than one page. As you can see in Figure 1.12, the preview screen shows the number of pages in the printed area.

If the message at the lower left of the preview screen shows that more than one page will print, restoring the form to a single page may be as simple as adjusting the margins. Just click the Margins button in the Toolbar of the preview screen, and adjust them. Figure 1.12 shows a form in which the top margin is so large that it is forcing a second page. By clicking the Zoom and Margin buttons, you can fine tune the form and print it on a single page.

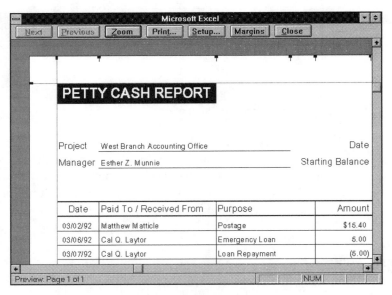

Figure 1.12 A zoomed preview screen.

All the files in *Winning Forms for Microsoft Excel* use margins that enable you to print them on any printer. In general, margins are at least 0.5 inches in any dimension. A few forms use even wider margins. Some printers will support narrower margins in all dimensions. Check your printer documentation for the margins it will support, and try changing them if the margins in the form are too wide and changing the form forces it to print on more than one page. For example, if you use a Hewlett-Packard LaserJet, you can make any margin as narrow as 0.25 inches. If you make the margin narrower, Excel will attempt to print in the non-printing area of the paper. The result will be truncated text. Choose the File Page Setup (or type [Alt]FT) to change margins. Enter the margin size you want to use in the Margins text boxes. If that solves the problem, and you like the way the form looks, fine.

If changing the margins does not solve the problem, consider using the print scaling feature of Excel. That is, choose File Page Setup and choose the Fit to or Reduce/Enlarge features. The disadvantage to scaling the document to print it on one page is that it changes both the length and width of form. If your only problem is that one or two lines have spilled over to a second page, scaling may make the form too narrow.

On occasion, making a change in a form may create a second (or even a third and fourth page) that contains no text. Should that happen, and you determine that there really is no text on the subsequent pages, you can solve the problem simply by instructing Excel to print only the first page of the print area. That is, after you choose File Print, click Pages in the Print Range box, and enter 1 in the From and To boxes.

Adding a Logo

A number of forms are designed to be used as public documents and contain a shaded area where you can add a logo. Such a form is shown in Figure 1.13. Whenever a form contains such an area, it is unprotected and you can insert a logo without first unprotecting the file. If you decide to add a logo to a form that does not contain a space for one, you must first choose Options Unprotect Document, or type [Alt]OP.

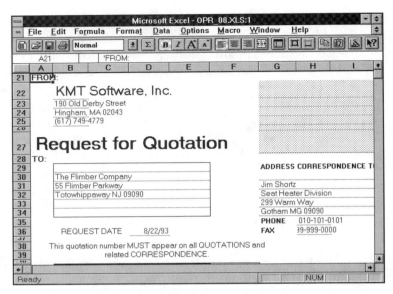

Figure 1.13 A form to which you can add a logo.

To add the logo, open the application (a painting or drawing program, for example) and then open the file that contains the graphic you want to use. Select the graphic, if necessary, and copy it to the clipboard. (Or choose Copy from the Edit menu.) Then return to Excel and paste the graphic into the worksheet by choosing Paste from the Edit menu. Figures 1.13 and 1.14 show a form before and after adding a graphic. Once the graphic has been placed in the worksheet, you can resize it to cover the shaded area.

You cannot change the format, font, pattern, of any cell (even those into which you enter data) without first choosing Options Unprotect Document, nor can you insert or delete any rows or columns in the worksheet. Thus, once you have removed protection from the file, take care that you do not unintentionally erase or alter any formulas that a Winning Form might depend upon.

Deleting Rows and Columns in a Form

Before you delete any row or column in a file, make doubly sure that you can do so without serious consequences. Many forms will still print properly if you delete or insert a row or column, some may not.

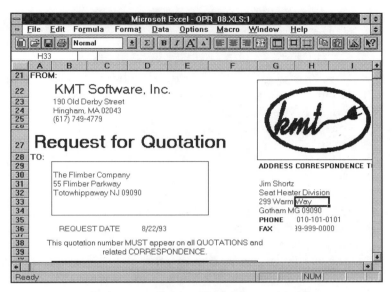

Figure 1.14 The same form with the logo added.

Obviously, you should avoid deleting any rows or columns that would create an error condition in the form. If you inadvertently create an error, however, you may be able to spot it quickly in the zoomed file and recover by invoking Undo. That is, by pressing Ctrl Z.

If you decide to change the width of any columns, however, you may have to change several printer settings, particularly the margins. Once again, use the File Print Preview command to determine whether you will have to make any adjustments. Don't forget that when you are in Preview mode in Excel, you can click the Margins button, and change margins to fit the form on a single page.

If you are particularly adept at using Excel, you can even link the forms to other Excel files or add more material to the files we supply to create an entire small business planning and financial system.

Spreadsheet Publishing and Forms

Winning Forms for Microsoft Excel exploits the spreadsheet publishing capabilities of Excel. While you might use Excel for many of the same tasks even if it did not contain text alignment commands or the ability to add borders to cells, or select several fonts, those are crucial elements in the design of a form. In this section we will share a few helpful techniques you may use when you design forms of your own.

The simplest way to align text in a cell is by clicking the right, left, or center aligning tools in the Toolbar. Choose Format Alignment Center across selection. Occasionally, however, the text still does not align as you wish. Figure 1.15 shows two alignment examples (for purposes of this illustration, we have made the gridlines visible in the form). Notice that the cell pointer in the figure is in cell G26 and that the text, which is much wider than the cell that contains it. That is, if the cell is narrower than the text, the text will extend beyond both borders of the cell, displaying evenly on each side, assuming the cells on either side are empty. Just below the form title in Figure 1.15, in cells H28..H32, is a series of labels that are aligned to the right side of the cells that contain them, and have the effect of pointing to the data entry cells on their right. Notice cell H29 in particular. Its text extends into the cell to its left (G29) while lining up on the right with the text above and below it.

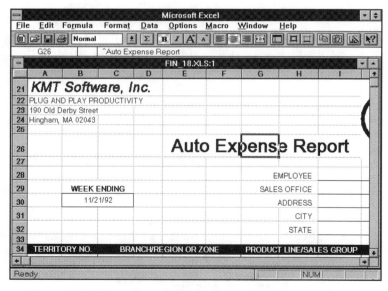

Figure 1.15 Examples of alignment in a form.

CHAPTER

2

ADMINISTRATIVE FORMS

The forms in this chapter include a series of calendars and time planning forms, and such forms as appointment schedules, memos, and faxes. In general, these forms are designed to help you control and manage such tasks as time planning, travel, simple schedules, and simple communications.

Yearly Calendar

Disk File Name

ADM_01.XLS

Using This Form

Use this file to create a yearly calendar. You can apply shading to important dates, and you can add a custom title by entering text into row 26 [1].

Entering Data

The only data that has to be entered is the year. Enter it in cell E19 (not shown in the illustration). If you enter four digits for the year, it may appear on your screen as a series of asterisks, but the calendar will calculate correctly. You can enter any year between 1900 and 2078; any other year will produce a calendar, but it may be incorrect.

Printing This Form

Click the printer tool in the toolbar or choose Print from the File menu.

Adapting This Form

If you want to distribute this calendar to customers, you may wish to expand the print area (using Options Set Print Area) and add your business name, address, and telephone number at the bottom. After you print the blank form, take it to a printer and print several hundred on heavy or colored stock. Or, if you do not want to use heavy stock, just print it on your laser using colored stock.

1992

SELLING THROUGH IN '92

JANUARY
S	M	T	W	T	F	S
			1	2	3	4
5	6	7	8	9	10	11
12	13	14	15	16	17	18
19	20	21	22	23	24	25
26	27	28	29	30	31	

FEBRUARY
S	M	T	W	T	F	S
						1
2	3	4	5	6	7	8
9	10	11	12	13	14	15
16	17	18	19	20	21	22
23	24	25	26	27	28	29

MARCH
S	M	T	W	T	F	S
1	2	3	4	5	6	7
8	9	10	11	12	13	14
15	16	17	18	19	20	21
22	23	24	25	26	27	28
29	30	31				

APRIL
S	M	T	W	T	F	S
			1	2	3	4
5	6	7	8	9	10	11
12	13	14	15	16	17	18
19	20	21	22	23	24	25
26	27	28	29	30		

MAY
S	M	T	W	T	F	S
					1	2
3	4	5	6	7	8	9
10	11	12	13	14	15	16
17	18	19	20	21	22	23
24	25	26	27	28	29	30
31						

JUNE
S	M	T	W	T	F	S
	1	2	3	4	5	6
7	8	9	10	11	12	13
14	15	16	17	18	19	20
21	22	23	24	25	26	27
28	29	30				

JULY
S	M	T	W	T	F	S
			1	2	3	4
5	6	7	8	9	10	11
12	13	14	15	16	17	18
19	20	21	22	23	24	25
26	27	28	29	30	31	

AUGUST
S	M	T	W	T	F	S
						1
2	3	4	5	6	7	8
9	10	11	12	13	14	15
16	17	18	19	20	21	22
23	24	25	26	27	28	29
30	31					

SEPTEMBER
S	M	T	W	T	F	S
		1	2	3	4	5
6	7	8	9	10	11	12
13	14	15	16	17	18	19
20	21	22	23	24	25	26
27	28	29	30			

OCTOBER
S	M	T	W	T	F	S
				1	2	3
4	5	6	7	8	9	10
11	12	13	14	15	16	17
18	19	20	21	22	23	24
25	26	27	28	29	30	31

NOVEMBER
S	M	T	W	T	F	S
1	2	3	4	5	6	7
8	9	10	11	12	13	14
15	16	17	18	19	20	21
22	23	24	25	26	27	28
29	30					

DECEMBER
S	M	T	W	T	F	S
		1	2	3	4	5
6	7	8	9	10	11	12
13	14	15	16	17	18	19
20	21	22	23	24	25	26
27	28	29	30	31		

Yearly Planner

Disk File Name

ADM_02.XLS

Using This Form

Use this calendar to outline your plans and goals for a full year. Like the other calendars in Winning Forms, this is "live," and can be used for many years. Use the notepad area at the bottom of the sheet to record your ideas about accomplishing the goals you enter into the planning boxes.

Entering Data

You can type in the goal planning boxes [1], or the notepad [2], or you can fill in the form by hand. Enter the year in the cell Y19 (not shown in the illustration), either as a full year or the final two digits.

Printing This Form

Click the printer tool in the toolbar or choose Print from the File menu.

Adapting This Form

If you prefer a landscape version of this form, use File Page Setup to change the orientation. Then change column AA to 30 characters (using Format Column Width, or by dragging the column border to the right). Finally, redefine the print area (using Options Set Print Area) to end on row 67. Before printing, take a look at the form using File Print Preview.

1993 PLANNING CALENDAR

JANUARY
S	M	T	W	T	F	S
					1	2
3	4	5	6	7	8	9
10	11	12	13	14	15	16
17	18	19	20	21	22	23
24	25	26	27	28	29	30
31						

FEBRUARY
S	M	T	W	T	F	S
	1	2	3	4	5	6
7	8	9	10	11	12	13
14	15	16	17	18	19	20
21	22	23	24	25	26	27
28						

MARCH
S	M	T	W	T	F	S
	1	2	3	4	5	6
7	8	9	10	11	12	13
14	15	16	17	18	19	20
21	22	23	24	25	26	27
28	29	30	31			

APRIL
S	M	T	W	T	F	S
				1	2	3
4	5	6	7	8	9	10
11	12	13	14	15	16	17
18	19	20	21	22	23	24
25	26	27	28	29	30	

MAY
S	M	T	W	T	F	S
						1
2	3	4	5	6	7	8
9	10	11	12	13	14	15
16	17	18	19	20	21	22
23	24	25	26	27	28	29
30	31					

JUNE
S	M	T	W	T	F	S
		1	2	3	4	5
6	7	8	9	10	11	12
13	14	15	16	17	18	19
20	21	22	23	24	25	26
27	28	29	30			

JULY
S	M	T	W	T	F	S
				1	2	3
4	5	6	7	8	9	10
11	12	13	14	15	16	17
18	19	20	21	22	23	24
25	26	27	28	29	30	31

AUGUST
S	M	T	W	T	F	S
1	2	3	4	5	6	7
8	9	10	11	12	13	14
15	16	17	18	19	20	21
22	23	24	25	26	27	28
29	30	31				

SEPTEMBER
S	M	T	W	T	F	S
			1	2	3	4
5	6	7	8	9	10	11
12	13	14	15	16	17	18
19	20	21	22	23	24	25
26	27	28	29	30		

OCTOBER
S	M	T	W	T	F	S
					1	2
3	4	5	6	7	8	9
10	11	12	13	14	15	16
17	18	19	20	21	22	23
24	25	26	27	28	29	30
31						

NOVEMBER
S	M	T	W	T	F	S
	1	2	3	4	5	6
7	8	9	10	11	12	13
14	15	16	17	18	19	20
21	22	23	24	25	26	27
28	29	30				

DECEMBER
S	M	T	W	T	F	S
			1	2	3	4
5	6	7	8	9	10	11
12	13	14	15	16	17	18
19	20	21	22	23	24	25
26	27	28	29	30	31	

PERSONAL GOALS

Lose 20 pounds by July 1

Get finances in order

Buy new car

Fix the slice

And the hook

❶

BUSINESS GOALS

Earn a better territory

Sell 150% of last year

Open 24 new accounts

❶

❷

Quarterly Planner

Disk File Name

ADM_03.XLS

Using This Form

This form permits you to plan a full quarter. You can set the quarter to begin in any month of the year, and view a calendar covering that quarter. The year shown in the small calendar is always the calendar year.

Entering Data

Type your plans and goals in the notepad section [1], or fill in items by hand. Enter values for the quarter and year in row 19 (you may enter the full year or just the final two digits). Enter a month for the start of the fiscal year as a numeral or by name.

Printing This Form

Click the printer tool in the toolbar or choose Print from the File menu.

Adapting This Form

If you would like to use this planner in landscape format, use File Page Setup to change the orientation. Then reset column R (or any other column except Q, which contains the data entry cell for the year) to 32 characters (using Format Column Width, or by dragging the column border to the right). You should then change the print area (using Options Set Print Area) to A21..X63. Before printing, take a look at the form using File Print Preview.

First Quarter 1993

JAN 1993						
S	M	T	W	T	F	S
					1	2
3	4	5	6	7	8	9
10	11	12	13	14	15	16
17	18	19	20	21	22	23
24	25	26	27	28	29	30
31						

Put together proposal for Flimber company (why did they

name it that?) by Jan 24

Ship date for flounder platter mold is 1/31   ❶

Fred F, birthday, 1/17

FEB 1993						
S	M	T	W	T	F	S
	1	2	3	4	5	6
7	8	9	10	11	12	13
14	15	16	17	18	19	20
21	22	23	24	25	26	27
28						

Wilma's birthday 2/7

MAR 1993						
S	M	T	W	T	F	S
	1	2	3	4	5	6
7	8	9	10	11	12	13
14	15	16	17	18	19	20
21	22	23	24	25	26	27
28	29	30	31			

Overall this quarter we have to finish development of the hash thrashers!

Monthly Calendar

Disk File Name

ADM_04.XLS

Using This Form

This form produces a monthly calendar for printing in landscape mode. The calendar shows the dates and the day of the year for each day. If you like, you can apply shading (using Format Patterns Pattern) to special dates in the month.

Entering Data

Enter the month and year you want in B19 and E19 (not shown), respectively. If you enter *This, Last,* or *Next* in B19, the calendar will use the current year and month as a basis, regardless of the entry in E19. You can use the number of a month or the first three letters of its name.

Printing This Form

Click the printer tool in the toolbar or choose Print from the File menu.

Adapting This Form

For a five-day, business week calendar, change columns C, E, G, I, and K to 15 or 16 characters, then change the print area to C21..L61. You cannot get more than 16 characters in the day columns without changing the print margins. You will probably also want to move item numbers in the Plans for Next Month section [1], and to adjust lines in the Special Dates [2] at the top.

Notice that each day in the calendar shows the day of the year. If you wish, you can modify the formula that returns that data to show the number of days remaining in the year.

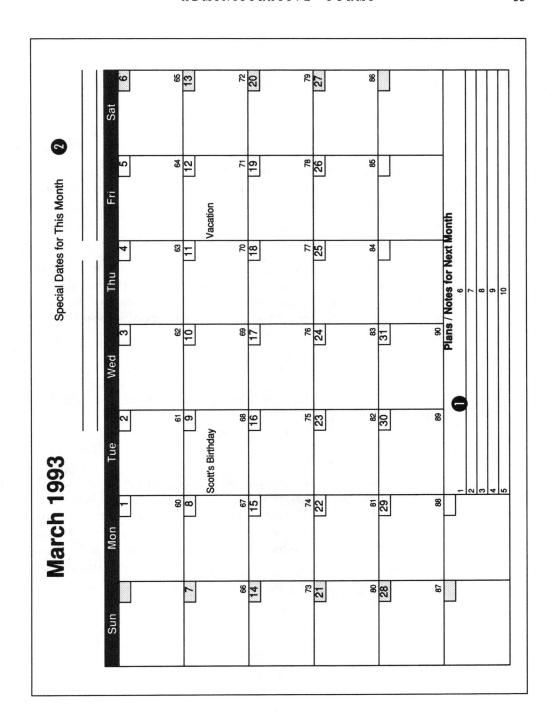

March 1993

Special Dates for This Month ❷

Sun	Mon	Tue	Wed	Thu	Fri	Sat
	1	2	3	4	5	6
7	8	9 Scott's Birthday	10	11	12	13
14	15	16	17	18	Vacation 19	20
21	22	23	24	25	26	27
28	29	30	31			

❶

Plans / Notes for Next Month

1
2
3
4
5
6
7
8
9
10

Monthly Calendar 2

Disk File Name

ADM_05.XLS

Using This Form

This form produces a monthly calendar for printing in portrait mode. The calendar shows the dates as well as the day of the year for each day.

Entering Data

Enter the month and year you want in C19 and G19 (not shown in the illustration). If you enter *This*, *Last*, or *Next* in C19, the calendar will use the current year and month as a basis, regardless of the entry in G19. You can also enter the first three letters of a month or its number.

Printing This Form

Click the printer tool in the toolbar or choose Print from the File menu.

Adapting This Form

For a five-day, business week calendar, change columns C, E, G, I, and K to 10 or 12 characters, then change the print area to C21..L69. If you use 12 characters in the day columns you may have to change the right margin to print the right border on the days. You will probably also want to move item numbers in the Plans for Next Month section [1], and to adjust lines in the Special Dates section [2] at the top.

April 1993

Special Dates for This Month ❷

_____ _____
_____ _____

Sun	Mon	Tue	Wed	Thu	Fri	Sat
				1	2	3
				91	92	93
4	5	6	7	8	9	10
94	95	96	97	98	99	100
11	12	13	14	15	16	17
101	102	103	104	105	106	107
18	19	20	21	22	23	24
108	109	110	111	112	113	114
25	26	27	28	29	30	
115	116	117	118	119	120	

Plans / Notes for Next Month ❶

1	7
2	8
3	9
4	10
5	11
6	12

Daily Planner

Disk File Name

ADM_06.XLS

Using This Form

You can print this planning form only for the days you need one, or you can print a form for each day of the month, insert them in a ring binder, and have a monthly schedule. Just enter 1 in cell M19, and print the calendar. After the first planner page prints, change M19 to 2 and print again.

Entering Data

Enter data in the various areas either in the worksheet or by hand. To create a planner for a single day, enter the year, month, and day in cells D19, H19, and M19, respectively. If you enter four digits for the year, cell D19 will display a series of number signs, but the calendar will calculate correctly. For years after 1999, use four digits.

Printing This Form

Click the printer tool in the toolbar or choose Print from the File menu.

Adapting This Form

If you want to print a month's worth of daily planners, you can do so using a macro. Such a macro looks like this:

```
PRINT_MONTH =SET.VALUE(STOP_PRINT,'C:\WF\ADM_06.XLS'!days,0) =
FOR("COUNT_DAYS",1,STOP_PRINT,1)
   =PRINT(1,1,1,1,FALSE,FALSE,1,)
   =NEXT()
   =RETURN()
   =HALT()
STOP_PRINT    28
```

Enter the macro in a macro worksheet and select the range that contains the macro code, and the labels that identify the ranges STOP_PRINT andPRINT_MACRO. Then choose Formula Create Names and check the Left Column box to name the ranges. To run it, choose Macro Run, select PRINT_MONTH, and click OK.

Friday, FEBRUARY 12, 1993

Day 43   322 Days Remaining

REMINDERS FOR TODAY

Valentine's Day card for MCL and send flowers

HR	DONE	MTGS / APPTS	PRIORITY A,B,C	CALLS	PRIORITY A,B,C	NOTES
7						
8						
9		Jim & Scott @ Derby Street	A+			
10						
11						
12		Lunch / Steve Cosmopulo	A			
1						
2		Production Meeting	A			Remember slide show
3		Production Meeting Production Meeting				
4		Production Meeting				Time for look
5		Larry M?	B	Jeff Craig	A	at new product?
6				Jim		
7		Nick Amdur - 50th Bday				
8						

JANUARY						
S	M	T	W	T	F	S
					1	2
3	4	5	6	7	8	9
10	11	12	13	14	15	16
17	18	19	20	21	22	23
24	25	26	27	28	29	30
31						

FEBRUARY						
S	M	T	W	T	F	S
	1	2	3	4	5	6
7	8	9	10	11	12	13
14	15	16	17	18	19	20
21	22	23	24	25	26	27
28						

MARCH						
S	M	T	W	T	F	S
	1	2	3	4	5	6
7	8	9	10	11	12	13
14	15	16	17	18	19	20
21	22	23	24	25	26	27
28	29	30	31			

EXPENSES

ITEM	AMOUNT	REASON	TAX
Lunch SC		Flimber account status	Y

One Year Project Progress

Disk File Name

ADM_07.XLS

Using This Form

This form is designed to help you track various phases of a project. Enter actual or estimated completion dates—or key milestones—in the various columns associated with each phase of the project.

Entering Data

Enter the project name and start date in the spaces provided [1]. Then enter the project details into the other unprotected cells. Change the starting month by typing the first three letters of the month in cell D29 [2] (for example JAN). The other months will be calculated automatically by formulas.

Printing This Form

Click the printer tool in the toolbar or choose Print from the File menu.

ONE YEAR PROJECT PROGRESS

❶ PROJECT Roller Skating Rink Campaign

START DATE September 30, 1992

❷

PHASE DESCRIPTION	PERSON/DEPT RESPONSIBLE	JAN	FEB	MAR	APR	MAY	JUN	JUL	AUG	SEP	OCT	NOV	DEC
Organize Advertising	M. Barris	10/15											
Design Package	Phil Debochs			12/30									
Find Financing	M.T. Ouellette		11/21										
Get Contracts	Hugh Bett				1/3								

Appointments

Disk File Name

ADM_08.XLS

Using This Form

This form is used for scheduling appointments or other events in a five-day week. It produces the appropriate day of the week based on the date you use. The hours shown are unprotected, so you can change them to suit your needs. If you do, you may have to relocate the heavy lines that outline the noon hour.

Entering Data

Enter the date you want to use for the first day of the form in cell C19 (not shown in the illustration). The easiest date to use is in the format mm/dd/yy. However, whichever format you choose, make sure you use one that Excel recognizes as a date.

Printing This Form

Click the printer tool in the toolbar or choose Print from the File menu.

Adapting This Form

You could use this form as a schedule for meeting rooms or classes. Simply change the heading in A21 [1].

Appointments ❶

Time	MONDAY 05/10/93	TUESDAY 05/11/93	WEDNESDAY 05/12/93	THURSDAY 05/13/93	FRIDAY 05/14/93
8:00			Breakfast / Jack Nevison		
8:30			@ Colonial Inn		
9:00					
9:30	Jim, Tim, Bill				
10:00				Steve Mintz re: his book	Mark Scapicchio
10:30		Dave Feldman re: Insur			
11:00					
11:30					
12:00		Peter Held @ Dorchester			
12:30		Yacht Club			
1:00			Group of 7 Meeting	Dan, Bob, Lisa @ Slate	
1:30					
2:00	Mike Mellin @ The Charles				
2:30		Mel Jones /CTI Proposal			
3:00					Vince Hennessy
3:30					
4:00					
4:30					
5:00					
5:30					
EVE					Dinner @ Jim & Carol's

Travel Itinerary

Disk File Name

ADM_09.XLS

Using This Form

This form summarizes your travel plans and lodging arrangements for one or more personal or business trips. It contains areas for flight information [1], auto rentals [2], and hotel reservations [3]. The numbers to the left of each flight indicate legs of a trip, not flight numbers. The "S" column [4] is optional, and contains the number of stops a flight makes.

Entering Data

Enter the flight and other travel data as labels . Enter the month and year for the calendar in cells D19 and G19 (not shown in the illustration).

Printing This Form

Click the printer tool in the toolbar or choose Print from the File menu.

Adapting This Form

Add your frequent flyer number or numbers for such things as airline travelers' and auto rental membership.

Travel Itinerary

February '93 through April '93   Name **Perry Patetick**

FEB '93						
S	M	T	W	T	F	S
	1	2	3	4	5	6
7	8	9	10	11	12	13
14	15	16	17	18	19	20
21	22	23	24	25	26	27
28						

MAR '93						
S	M	T	W	T	F	S
	1	2	3	4	5	6
7	8	9	10	11	12	13
14	15	16	17	18	19	20
21	22	23	24	25	26	27
28	29	30	31			

APR '93						
S	M	T	W	T	F	S
				1	2	3
4	5	6	7	8	9	10
11	12	13	14	15	16	17
18	19	20	21	22	23	24
25	26	27	28	29	30	

❶ FLIGHT INFORMATION

	DATE	DEPART	DESTINED	AIRLINE	FLIGHT #	LOCAL ARR TIME	S
1	11/25	1:45 p	Chicago	Untied	UN 9999	4:15 p	1
	CNNCT	5:45 p	Nankipoo	Oxcart	JBO99	9:38 p	2
2	11/28	3:50 p	Chicago	Oxcart	KT999	8:20 p	N
	CNNCT	9:45 p	Gotham	Uturn	UT9292	11:12 p	1
3	11/30	VAR	DC	Crump	SHUTTLE	VAR	N

❹ CAR RENTALS ❷

COMPANY	CONFIRM #
SHARPAY	H0909

❸ ACCOMMODATIONS

DATE	HOTEL	ADDRESS	PHONE
11/25	Le Floppiere	Downtown Flanipan	399-555-9999
11/27	Motel Forty-fore	44 Weenie Street	000-989-6543
11/28	Fleatime Arms	Park Avenue	212-555-5499

LOCAL CONTACTS

NAME & PHONE

Smitty Brothers, 999-9999

Lilly Padd, 555-9595

Vic Trolla, 959-0000

800 NUMBERS

AUTO RENTALS		HOTELS		AIRLINES	
Alamo	327-9633	Best Western	528-1234	American	433-7300
Avis	331-1212	Hilton	445-8667	Continental	231-0856
Budget	527-0700	Holiday Inn	465-4329	Delta	638-7333
Hertz	654-3131	Hyatt	233-1234	JAL	525-3663
National	227-7368	Marriott	228-9290	TWA	892-6398
Thrifty	367-2277	Sheraton	325-3535	United	241-6522
		Westin	228-3000	USAir	428-4322

Telephone Index

Disk File Name

ADM_10.XLS

Using This Form

The Telephone Index form will come in handy if you "turn over" your telephone contacts often or have to provide a telephone list for many people. Enter names using the last name first, and sort the range A25..I56 using A25 as the 1st key. That will give you a list of numbers alphabetized by name.

Entering Data

This form contains no formulas, so you can enter data in the worksheet, or print the worksheet and enter data manually.

Printing This Form

Click the printer tool in the toolbar or choose Print from the File menu.

Ellie Menterry, 5 Mar 93

TELEPHONE INDEX

NAME	ADDRESS	AREA	PHONE	EXT	FAX
O'Toole, Baghdad	55 Damascus St. Cairo, IL 09090	789	999-0000	8877	
McFeeney, Damascus	55 Baghdad St. Utica, NY 09090	789	999-0000		
McSwain, Manila	55 California St. Moscow, ID 90940	789	999-0000		
O'Sweeney, Paris	55 London St. Paris TX 09090	789	999-0000	8877	
Mullarney, Egypt	55 Bremerhaven Lane, Rome NY 40090	789	999-0000		

Telephone Message

Disk File Name

ADM_11.XLS

Using This Form

This form prints four telephone message forms on a page. It is particularly useful if you need only a few of these forms, or if you want to customize the message form for your office environment. Because part of the form is to be circled, you'll probably want to print it and use it on paper. Nevertheless, all data-entry areas are unprotected.

Entering Data

The checkbox descriptions [1] are easily customized for your particular needs. Simply type new descriptions (preceded by a space) in the unprotected cells in the first message form. Formulas in the other message forms will cause them to automatically reflect the text you've entered into the first. If you wish to use the forms in the worksheet, simply type data into unprotected cells.

Printing This Form

Click the printer tool in the toolbar or choose Print from the File menu.

TELEPHONE MESSAGE

For   Howell I. Noh

Mr.   Ms.   Mrs.   Dr.   Cora Spondent

Company

Phone #

☐ **❶** Called   ☐ Please Call Back

☐ Returned Your Call   [x] Will Call Back

☐ Left Voice Message ☐ Wants to See You

Message

Date   09/09/93   Time   02:25 PM

Signed

TELEPHONE MESSAGE

For

Mr.   Ms.   Mrs.   Dr.

Company

Phone #

☐ Called   ☐ Please Call Back

☐ Returned Your Call   ☐ Will Call Back

☐ Left Voice Message ☐ Wants to See You

Message

Date   Time

Signed

TELEPHONE MESSAGE

For

Mr.   Ms.   Mrs.   Dr.

Company

Phone #

☐ Called   ☐ Please Call Back

☐ Returned Your Call   ☐ Will Call Back

☐ Left Voice Message ☐ Wants to See You

Message

Date   Time

Signed

TELEPHONE MESSAGE

For

Mr.   Ms.   Mrs.   Dr.

Company

Phone #

☐ Called   ☐ Please Call Back

☐ Returned Your Call   ☐ Will Call Back

☐ Left Voice Message ☐ Wants to See You

Message

Date   Time

Signed

Cash Receipt

Disk File Name

ADM_12.XLS

Using This Form

Use this form when you want to give a receipt to a customer for cash received, or when you want to keep a receipt for cash disbursed. Except for the name, address, phone, and receipt number, this form is intended to be filled out on paper.

Entering Data

Enter your name and address (or the name and address of the person issuing the receipt) in the upper-left corner of the first receipt [1]. String formulas enable the other receipts to automatically display the same information. Enter a number in the first receipt [2] and formulas will cause the other receipts to be renumbered as well.

Printing This Form

Click the printer tool in the toolbar or choose Print from the File menu.

Ike & C. Clearly ❶
123 Carida Way
Zebedee, MS 98765
(999) 555-4567

CASH RECEIPT
Number ❷   101

Date _____

From _____ $ _____

Amount _____ Dollars

Purpose _____

☐ Cash   ☐ Check / Money Order   Signed _____

Ike & C. Clearly
123 Carida Way
Zebedee, MS 98765
(999) 555-4567

CASH RECEIPT
Number   102

Date _____

From _____ $ _____

Amount _____ Dollars

Purpose _____

☐ Cash   ☐ Check / Money Order   Signed _____

Ike & C. Clearly
123 Carida Way
Zebedee, MS 98765
(999) 555-4567

CASH RECEIPT
Number   103

Date _____

From _____ $ _____

Amount _____ Dollars

Purpose _____

☐ Cash   ☐ Check / Money Order   Signed _____

Petty Cash Report

Disk File Name

ADM_13.XLS

Using This Form

This form accounts for money deposited to and disbursed from a petty cash fund. As balances are calculated automatically, you can save time by maintaining this form electronically. However, it can also be used successfully on paper.

Entering Data

Enter the project and manager in the spaces provided, along with the beginning date. All dates [1] can be entered either as values or with the DATE function. Date cells use the mm/dd/yy format. Enter all other data in the unprotected cells provided. Enter disbursements [2] as positive numbers; [3] deposits as negative numbers.

Printing This Form

Click the printer tool in the toolbar or choose Print from the File menu.

Adapting This Form

You can use column D for account numbers or initials identifying the person authorizing the expense, if you wish. First, remove protection with Options Unprotect document, then add lines with Format Border, and enter account numbers or initials. Then use Format Cell Protection in cell D34 to enter the appropriate heading. You may have to adjust column widths to prevent the form from printing on two pages.

PETTY CASH REPORT

Project   West Branch Accounting Office   Date 03/01/92

Manager Esther Z. Munnie   Starting Balance $100.00

Date	Paid To / Received From	Purpose	Amount	Balance
03/02/92	Matthew Matticle	Postage	❷ $15.40	$84.60
03/06/92	Cal Q. Laytor	Emergency Loan	5.00	79.60
03/07/92	Cal Q. Laytor	Loan Repayment	❸ (5.00)	84.60
03/08/92	Dot Maytricks	Pencil Leads	12.43	72.17
03/09/92	Ty Priter	Milk & Sugar	4.97	67.20
03/09/92	P.C. Cloan	Note Pads, etc.	8.52	58.68
03/10/92	E. Z. Munnie	Deposit	(41.32)	100.00

Bank Reconciliation

Disk File Name

ADM_14.XLS

Using This Form

This form lets you reconcile your checkbook and bank statement. It can be used in paper or electronic form. The form includes sections for deposits made after the statement date, transfers into the account after the statement date, charges recorded after the statement date, and outstanding checks.

Entering Data

Enter your name [1], the bank [2], and the account number [3] in the spaces provided. Then enter the balances from your bank statement and checkbook [4]. If you have made deposits, transfers, and so forth [5] since the statement date, enter them in the applicable areas. Finally, enter outstanding checks into the area provided [6].

Printing This Form

Click the printer tool in the toolbar or choose Print from the File menu.

Bank Reconciliation

Month Apr-93

❶

Name Ty D. Summ

❷

Bank a/c Flybye-Knight S&L

❸

#673-56478329

Balance per Bank Statement	$15,649.34
Deposits After Statement Date	477.00
Transfers into Account After Statement Date	512.97
Charges Recorded After Statement Date	(358.50)
Outstanding Checks	(2,099.46)
Adjusted Balance per Bank Statement	$14,181.35
Balance per Checkbook or Ledger	$14,181.35
Difference	$0.00

❹

Deposits After Statement Date

Total $477.00

Description	Date	Amount	Description	Date	Amount
Anniversary Gift	04/12/93	50.00			
Tax Refund	04/14/93	427.00			

❺

Transfers into Account After Statement Date

Total $512.97

Description	Date	Amount	Description	Date	Amount
Transfer from Savings	04/12/93	500.00			
Interest	04/15/93	12.97			

Charges Recorded After Statement Date

Total $358.50

Description	Date	Amount	Description	Date	Amount
24 Hour Teller Charges	04/14/93	8.50			
Automatic Loan Pmt	04/15/93	350.00			

Outstanding Checks

Total $2,099.46

Description	Number	Amount	Description	Number	Amount
Bert's Beanery	1034	432.78			
Kit's Kitchen	1038	982.47			
Diane's Diner	1043	684.21			

❻

Fax Log

Disk File Name

ADM_15.XLS

Using This Form

Use this form to track both incoming and outgoing facsimile messages. The form provides space for the date, whether the fax was sent or received, the number of pages, the sender, the receiver, and the fax number. There are no calculations in the form, and since it should be kept near the fax machine, it may best be used on paper.

Entering Data

Either print the form and use it as is, or enter data into unprotected cells.

Printing This Form

Click the printer tool in the toolbar or choose Print from the File menu.

FAX LOG

Date	Sent	Rec'd	Pgs	Sender	Receiver	Number
20 Oct 92	X		3	Hugo First	Mr. E. Toomey	201-555-1212
29 Oct 92		X	4	KMT Software, Inc.	Eaton Runn	
29 Oct 92	X		2	Eaton Runn	KMT Software, Inc.	617-749-4299
03 Dec 92	X		1	Randy Udderway	Bill Zardu	212-555-1212
20 Jan 93		X	8	Doris Open	Mary O'Nett	

Memo

Disk File Name

ADM_16.XLS

Using This Form

This form is for simple one-page memos. Though Excel isn't the ideal environment for word processing, it is sometimes more convenient to create something in Excel than to load another program.

Entering Data

The memo header area (*To/From/Subject/Date*) contains unprotected cells. Simply enter text into these cells and then move the cell pointer to the main memo area, which also contains unprotected cells, where you may enter the rest of the text.

Printing This Form

Click the printer tool in the toolbar or choose Print from the File menu.

Adapting This Form

If you want to add a copies field to the memo, use cell H25. Just enter CC: (the cell and those to its right are not protected), make the cell bold by choosing using Format Font and clicking Bold in the Font Style text box or simply by clicking the bold tool in the toolbar. Then enter the names of those to whom you want to send copies.

MEMO

To: All Family and Friend Personnel

From: Shirley Ugest

Date: 25 November 1992

Subject: Past, Present, and Future Memorabilia   [Executive Directive #409]

Effective immediately, all memorabilia will be collected in the designated memo bins throughout the household premises and grounds. In this manner, we can assure that we retain all important knick-knacks, what-not, and trinkets.

Family members or friends caught violating this executive directive will lose their seniority in the circle of family or friends, respectively. They will also lose all rights to visitation of the said memorabilia for a period of one month, one week, and one day.

Two-Column Memo

Disk File Name

ADM_17.XLS

Using This Form

This form is for simple one-page memos. Though Excel isn't the ideal environment for word processing, it is sometimes more convenient to create something in Excel than to load another program. It is especially difficult to create two-column documents in some word processing packages. These are straightforward in Excel.

Entering Data

The memo header area on the left (*To/From/Date/Subject*) [1] contains unprotected cells. Simply enter text into these cells and then move the cell pointer to the right in order to access the main memo area [2]. This area also contains unprotected cells, into which the remaining text may be entered.

Printing This Form

Click the printer tool in the toolbar or choose Print from the File menu.

Memo

②

TO
Bea Leavitt, Ira Member

FROM
① Bertha Vanation, POLICY

DATE
October 20, 1992

SUBJECT
A Unanimous Declaration

When in the course of human events, it becomes necessary for one people to dissolve the political bands which have connected them with another, and to assume among the powers of the earth, the separate and equal station to which the Laws of Nature and of Nature's God entitle them, a decent respect to the opinions of mankind requires that they should declare the causes which impel them to the separation.

We hold these truths to be self-evident, that all men are created equal, that they are endowed by their Creator with certain unalienable Rights, that among these are Life, Liberty and the pursuit of Happiness. That to secure these rights, Governments are instituted among Men, deriving their just powers from the consent of the governed, That whenever any Form of Government becomes destructive of these ends, it is the Right of the People to alter or to abolish it, and to institute new Government, laying its foundation on such principles and organizing its powers in such form, as to them shall seem most likely to effect their Safety and Happiness.

Prudence, indeed, will dictate that Governments long established should not be changed for light and transient causes; and accordingly all experience hath shown, that mankind are more disposed to suffer, while evils are sufferable, than to right themselves by abolishing the forms to which they are accustomed. But when a long train of abuses and usurpations, pursuing invariably the same Object evinces a design to reduce them under absolute Despotism, it is their right, it is their duty, to throw off such Government, and to provide new Guards for their future security.

Such has been the patient sufferance of these Colonies; and such is now the necessity which constrains them to alter their former Systems of Government. The history of the present King of Great Britain is a history of repeated injuries and usurpations, all having in direct object the establishment of an absolute tyranny over these States. To prove this, let Facts be submitted to a candid world.

Fax Cover

Disk File Name

ADM_18.XLS

Using This Form

This form is a cover sheet to accompany facsimile transmissions. It indicates the sender, the person to whom it is addressed, the number of pages, and so on. The form may filled out on paper or electronically.

Entering Data

To create a master fax cover that can be filled out on paper, enter only the company name, address, and telephone number into the unprotected cells at the top of the form [1], then print it. To fill out the form electronically, simply enter the remaining information into the unprotected cells. A short memo may be added in the area below the box [2].

Printing This Form

Click the printer tool in the toolbar or choose Print from the File menu.

KMT Software, Inc.   190 Old Derby St, Hingham, MA 02043   617.749.4299

IMPORTANT FAX TRANSMISSION

To: Harry Moover, Natural Living, Inc.	❶
FAX #: 510.555.1212	Date: 18 February 1993
From: Tess T. Monial	Pages: 5
Subject: Please Expedite the Attached Contract	(including this cover)

Harry:

❷

As we discussed on the phone today, the attached pages represent the revised contract which we have been working on.

We would appreciate anything you can do to expedite the process through your legal department.

Thanks very much for your help. I will call in a day or two to see how things are proceeding.

- Tess

Two-Column Fax Cover

Disk File Name

ADM_19.XLS

Using This Form

This form is a cover sheet to accompany facsimile transmissions. It indicates the sender, the person to whom the fax is addressed, the number of pages, and so on. The form may filled out on paper or electronically.

Entering Data

To create a master fax cover that can be filled out on paper, enter only the company name, address, and telephone number into the unprotected cells at the left of the form [1], then print it. To fill out the form electronically, simply enter the remaining information into the unprotected cells. A short memo may be added on the right side of the page [2].

Printing This Form

Click the printer tool in the toolbar or choose Print from the File menu.

☎ FAX

COVER SHEET

FROM ❶
May B. Knott
KMT Software, Inc.
190 Old Derby Street
Hingham, MA 02043
(617) 749-4299

DELIVER TO
Izzy Hoam
F: (604) 555-1212
V: (604) 555-1212

SUBJECT
Facsimile Test

DATE
February 18, 1993

PAGES
Two
(including this cover)

❷

Izzy:

Thanks for agreeing to help me test my new FAX machine. I was really sold on its advanced scanning capabilities, so I hope it comes out looking really good.

Do be sure to give me a call to let me know how it came through. My voice phone is the same as the FAX phone; I have one of those auto-detection voice/data switches.

I'd also appreciate it if you could package up the FAX and mail it to me so I can see first-hand the quality of my new toy. Thanks again.

May B.

Seminar Evaluation

Disk File Name

ADM_20.XLS

Using This Form

This form can be used to evaluate presentations, seminars, and train-ing programs. It is intended to be customized, printed, and then filled out on paper.

Entering Data

Enter the title of the seminar [1] at the top of the form, then enter the names of the individual presentations [2] in the unprotected cells provided. Each evaluation line [3] can also be changed to suit your needs. Formulas cause the text entered in the first section to be re-flected in the other sections.

Printing This Form

Click the printer tool in the toolbar or choose Print from the File menu.

Seminar Evaluation   ❶ "Upscale Downsizing"

| strongly agree | | | | strongly disagree | ***Presentation 1*** *Corporate Corpulence*   ❷ |

5	4	3	2	1	> The presentation increased my subject knowledge.
5	4	3	2	1	> The presentation was professional and relevant. ❸
5	4	3	2	1	> I would recommend this presenter for future events.

Comments:

_____

_____

| strongly agree | | | | strongly disagree | ***Presentation 2*** *Cost-Saving Choices* |

5	4	3	2	1	> The presentation increased my subject knowledge.
5	4	3	2	1	> The presentation was professional and relevant.
5	4	3	2	1	> I would recommend this presenter for future events.

Comments:

_____

_____

| strongly agree | | | | strongly disagree | ***Presentation 3*** *Managing the Transition* |

5	4	3	2	1	> The presentation increased my subject knowledge.
5	4	3	2	1	> The presentation was professional and relevant.
5	4	3	2	1	> I would recommend this presenter for future events.

Comments:

_____

_____

CHAPTER
3

FINANCIAL FORMS

One of Excel's great strengths is how easy it makes financial analyses. This section contains a series of forms and reports designed to help you make professional-looking financial presentations.

The section also contains important external financial documents like invoices, expense report forms, and forms for reporting or recording automobile expenses.

Pro-Forma Balance Sheet

Disk File Name

FIN_01.XLS

Using This Form

This form is a financial planning tool for businesses. It is especially useful for estimating long-term financing needs. The form is best used in electronic form; however, like most Winning Forms, it can also be filled out on paper.

Entering Data

Enter data into the unprotected cells. The first year [1] is entered manually, but subsequent years are calculated by the form. The retained earnings figure [2] for each year is calculated, to insure that assets equal liabilities plus equity.

Printing This Form

Click the printer tool in the toolbar or choose Print from the File menu.

Pro-Forma Balance Sheet

Qumran Scrollwork, Inc.

For 1993 to 1996
(all numbers in $000)

❶

ASSETS	1993	1994	1995	1996
Current Assets				
Cash	$54	$57	$59	$64
Net accounts receivable	367	396	426	435
Inventory	177	191	203	205
Temporary investment	12	12	12	12
Prepaid expenses	2	2	2	2
Total Current Assets	$612	$658	$702	$718
Fixed Assets				
Long-term investments	$42	$43	$43	$46
Land	656	656	684	727
Buildings (net of depreciation)	903	928	983	1,021
Plant & equipment (net)	608	631	642	654
Furniture & fixtures (net)	61	65	68	72
Total Net Fixed Assets	$2,270	$2,323	$2,420	$2,520
TOTAL ASSETS	$2,882	$2,981	$3,122	$3,238
LIABILITIES				
Current Liabilities				
Accounts payable	$246	$252	$258	$277
Short-term notes	24	25	26	28
Current portion of long-term notes	14	14	14	15
Accruals & other payables	14	14	14	14
Total Current Liabilities	$298	$305	$312	$334
Long-term Liabilities				
Mortgage	$897	$931	$978	$1,021
Other long-term liabilities	443	485	527	576
Total Long-term Liabilities	$1,340	$1,416	$1,505	$1,597
Shareholders' Equity				
Capital stock	$300	$300	$300	$300
❷ Retained earnings	944	960	1,005	1,007
Total Shareholders' Equity	$1,244	$1,260	$1,305	$1,307
TOTAL LIABILITIES & EQUITY	$2,882	$2,981	$3,122	$3,238

Balance Sheet

Disk File Name

FIN_02.XLS

Using This Form

This form is a financial report for businesses. It is primarily used for reporting the firm's financial condition to owners. It is also presented to lenders to obtain financing. The form can be filled out either on paper or electronically.

Entering Data

Enter data into the unprotected cells. The retained earnings figure [1] for each year is calculated, to insure that assets equal liabilities plus equity. Please note that doubtful accounts [2] and accumulated depreciation [3] must be entered as negative numbers.

Printing This Form

Click the printer tool in the toolbar or choose Print from the File menu.

Balance Sheet

General Certification, Inc.

For Year Ending June 1992
(all numbers in $000)

ASSETS

Current Assets

Cash	$51
Accounts receivable	340
(less doubtful accounts) **2**	(129)
Inventory	175
Temporary investment	12
Prepaid expenses	2
Total Current Assets	**$451**

Fixed Assets

Long-term investments	$40
Land	650
Buildings	841
(less accumulated depreciation) **3**	(132)
Plant & equipment	560
(less accumulated depreciation)	(331)
Furniture & fixtures	57
(less accumulated depreciation)	(41)
Total Net Fixed Assets	**$1,644**

TOTAL ASSETS	**$2,095**

LIABILITIES

Current Liabilities

Accounts payable	$237
Short-term notes	23
Current portion of long-term notes	14
Interest payable	5
Taxes payable	10
Accrued payroll	13
Total Current Liabilities	**$302**

Long-term Liabilities

Mortgage	$840
Other long-term liabilities	425
Total Long-term Liabilities	**$1,265**

Shareholders' Equity

Capital stock	$300
1 Retained earnings	228
Total Shareholders' Equity	**$528**

TOTAL LIABILITIES & EQUITY	**$2,095**

Pro-Forma Income Statement

Disk File Name

FIN_03.XLS

Using This Form

This form is a financial planning tool for businesses. It is especially useful for estimating long-term financing needs. The form is best used in electronic form; however, like most Winning Forms, it can also be filled out on paper.

Entering Data

Enter data into the unprotected cells. The first year is entered manually [1]; subsequent years are calculated by the form.

Printing This Form

Click the printer tool in the toolbar or choose Print from the File menu.

Pro-Forma Income Statement

HNT Marine, Inc.

For Period Ending February 1993

(all numbers in $000)

❶

	1993	1994	1995	1996
REVENUE				
Gross sales	$500	$650	$720	$850
Less sales returns and allowances	200	230	280	320
Net Sales	$300	$420	$440	$530
COST OF SALES				
Beginning inventory	$350	$360	$420	$435
Plus goods purchased / manufactured	120	165	185	190
Total Goods Available	$470	$525	$605	$625
Less ending inventory	360	420	435	440
Total Cost of Goods Sold	$110	$105	$170	$185
Gross Profit (Loss)	$190	$315	$270	$345
OPERATING EXPENSES				
Selling				
Salaries and wages	$35	$41	$46	$52
Commissions	12	14	16	18
Advertising	10	12	14	20
Depreciation	14	15	16	16
Other	5	6	6	7
Total Selling Expenses	$76	$88	$98	$113
General/Administrative				
Salaries and wages	$12	$14	$16	$18
Employee benefits	4	5	5	6
Payroll taxes	2	3	3	4
Insurance	6	6	7	7
Rent	8	8	9	9
Utilities	2	2	2	3
Depreciation & amortization	3	4	4	5
Office supplies	1	1	1	1
Travel & entertainment	3	3	3	4
Postage	1	1	1	2
Equipment maintenance & rental	0	0	1	1
Interest	0	1	1	2
Furniture & equipment	3	4	4	5
Total General/Administrative Expenses	$45	$52	$57	$67
Total Operating Expenses	$121	$140	$155	$180
Net Income Before Taxes	$69	$175	$115	$165
Taxes on income	22	32	26	28
Net Income After Taxes	$47	$143	$89	$137
Extraordinary gain or loss	$0	$0	$43	$0
Income tax on extraordinary gain	0	0	12	0
NET INCOME (LOSS)	$47	$143	$120	$137

Income Statement

Disk File Name

FIN_04.XLS

Using This Form

This form is a financial report for businesses. It is primarily used to report the condition of the firm to management and ownership. It is also presented to lenders to obtain financing. Due to the large number of calculations, the form is best filled out electronically; however, like most Winning Forms, it can also be filled out on paper.

Entering Data

Enter data for the current month [1] and the year to date [2] into the unprotected cells of the form. The form automatically calculates each line item as a percentage of net sales.

Printing This Form

Click the printer tool in the toolbar or choose Print from the File menu.

Income Statement

HNT Marine, Inc.

For Period Ending February 1993
(all numbers in $000)

	❶ Current Month		**❷ Year to Date**	
	Amount	% of Sales	Amount	% of Sales
REVENUE				
Gross Sales	$500		$2,500	
Less sales returns and allowances	200		500	
Net Sales	$300	100%	$2,000	100%
COST OF SALES				
Beginning inventory	$350	117%	$240	12%
Plus goods purchased / manufactured	120	40%	900	45%
Total Goods Available	$470	157%	$1,140	57%
Less ending inventory	360	120%	360	18%
Total Cost of Goods Sold	$110	37%	$780	39%
Gross Profit (Loss)	$190	63%	$1,220	61%
OPERATING EXPENSES				
Selling				
Salaries and wages	$35	12%	$130	7%
Commissions	12	4%	80	4%
Advertising	10	3%	60	3%
Depreciation	14	5%	120	6%
Other	5	2%	30	2%
Total Selling Expenses	$76	25%	$420	21%
General/Administrative				
Salaries and wages	$12	4%	$130	7%
Employee benefits	3	1%	31	2%
Payroll taxes	2	1%	23	1%
Insurance	2	1%	1	0%
Rent	12	4%	23	1%
Utilities	2	1%	30	2%
Depreciation & amortization	1	0%	16	1%
Office supplies	1	0%	8	0%
Travel & entertainment	2	1%	4	0%
Postage	1	0%	11	1%
Equipment maintenance & rental	4	1%	49	2%
Interest	2	1%	31	2%
Furniture & equipment	1	0%	10	1%
Total General/Administrative Expenses	$45	15%	$367	18%
Total Operating Expenses	$121	40%	$787	39%
Net Income Before Taxes	$69	23%	$433	22%
Taxes on income	22	7%	135	7%
Net Income After Taxes	$47	16%	$411	21%
Extraordinary gain or loss	$0	0%	$0	0%
Income tax on extraordinary gain	0	0%	0	0%
NET INCOME (LOSS)	$47	16%	$411	21%

Five Year Projections

Disk File Name

FIN_05.XLS

Using This Form

This form projects the key financial figures for a company over five years. The projections include abbreviated income and cash flow statements, and a balance sheet.

Entering Data

Enter all data into unprotected cells. Enter the date [1] in the space provided. The cell that contains the first year [2] is unprotected. Enter the beginning year into this cell, and the others will be calculated automatically. Please note that the entry cells for cash outflow (cells C41..G41) [3] require negative numbers.

Printing This Form

Click the printer tool in the toolbar or choose Print from the File menu.

KMT Manufacturing, Inc.
Five Year Projections

❶ 31 December 1992

	❷ 1993	1994	1995	1996	1997
Income Statement					
Net sales	$43,300	$67,900	$77,300	$80,200	$88,100
Cost of goods sold	24,100	24,600	20,800	21,900	39,500
Net Operating Income	$19,200	$43,300	$56,500	$58,300	$48,600
Operating expenses	3,500	3,900	2,100	3,000	3,600
Net Income	$15,700	$39,400	$54,400	$55,300	$45,000
Cash Flow Statement					
Beginning balance	$24,500	$22,300	$18,200	$18,900	$21,600
Cash inflow	7,000	7,600	9,400	9,900	7,000
Cash outflow	❸ (8,200)	(5,400)	(6,900)	(7,900)	(8,900)
Ending Cash Balance	$23,300	$24,500	$20,700	$20,900	$19,700
Balance Sheet					
Cash	$6,800	$7,200	$6,400	$8,600	$14,000
Accounts receivable	17,600	13,800	19,800	19,500	21,800
Inventory	6,300	8,200	9,300	9,400	11,200
Prepaid expenses	5,700	6,300	5,800	3,200	2,700
Total Current Assets	$36,400	$35,500	$41,300	$40,700	$49,700
Fixed assets	28,000	30,500	45,000	43,000	41,000
Total Assets	$64,400	$66,000	$86,300	$83,700	$90,700
Accounts payable	$6,400	$6,200	$9,800	$7,600	$8,200
Short-term notes	5,700	5,500	4,800	5,400	7,700
Accrued & other liabilities	2,300	2,300	3,000	2,900	2,700
Total Current Liabilities	$14,400	$14,000	$17,600	$15,900	$18,600
Long-term debt	$22,100	$23,700	$22,600	$21,800	$24,900
Other long-term liabilities	1,400	1,800	1,400	1,000	1,700
Total Long-term Liabilities	$23,500	$25,500	$24,000	$22,800	$26,600
Shareholders' equity	$26,500	$26,500	$44,700	$45,000	$45,500
Total Liabilities and Equity	$64,400	$66,000	$86,300	$83,700	$90,700

G&A Expense Budget

Disk File Name

FIN_06.XLS

Using This Form

This form compares actual General and Administrative (G&A) expenses with budgeted amounts for the current month and the year to date. Fixed expenses generally do not change over the course of the year, while variable expenses change with the level of activity.

You will note that some of the expenses (such as postage and telephone) are listed under both the fixed and variable categories. This is a common accounting practice that separates the minimum bill or fixed expense you must pay for telephone service or postage meters, and the part of the expense line or variable expense over and above the minimum expense that changes from month to month—for example, the number of long distance phone calls or the amount of postage you used.

Entering Data

Enter data into unprotected cells. Variances and totals are calculated automatically.

Printing This Form

Click the printer tool in the toolbar or choose Print from the File menu.

G&A Expense Budget

Colonel Kernel Popping Corn, Inc.

For Period Ending June, 1993

	This Month			Year to Date		
	Budget	Actual	Variance	Budget	Actual	Variance
FIXED						
Exec salaries	$3,200	$1,900	($1,300)	$31,100	$46,600	$15,500
Office salaries	13,900	8,700	(5,200)	36,400	45,100	8,700
Employee benefits	22,900	19,800	(3,100)	226,600	259,000	32,400
Payroll taxes	14,200	7,500	(6,700)	28,900	41,800	12,900
Travel and entertainment	4,100	5,100	1,000	15,100	20,000	4,900
Directors' fees and expense:	38,400	36,100	(2,300)	187,300	167,800	(19,500)
Insurance	18,600	10,000	(8,600)	64,100	58,200	(5,900)
Rent	47,500	49,700	2,200	377,500	333,300	(44,200)
Depreciation	46,600	30,200	(16,400)	334,000	201,400	(132,600)
Taxes	40,400	59,900	19,500	415,900	404,600	(11,300)
Legal	28,200	31,200	3,000	214,800	193,900	(20,900)
Audit	10,600	11,800	1,200	87,200	104,100	16,900
Telephone	15,500	10,300	(5,200)	15,200	21,400	6,200
Utilities	31,000	39,300	8,300	68,000	97,400	29,400
Contributions	36,500	43,700	7,200	87,900	92,100	4,200
Postage	27,300	30,500	3,200	130,400	161,900	31,500
Dues	21,300	30,800	9,500	142,100	180,700	38,600
Sundry	14,800	20,300	5,500	91,000	97,800	6,800
VARIABLE						
Office salaries	23,000	32,400	9,400	53,000	29,500	(23,500)
Employee benefits	29,800	27,800	(2,000)	292,600	170,200	(122,400)
Payroll taxes	4,700	3,300	(1,400)	14,400	17,100	2,700
Travel and entertainment	36,100	53,400	17,300	111,400	108,900	(2,500)
Telephone and telegraph	4,600	6,300	1,700	47,500	44,300	(3,200)
Stationery and office supplie	6,600	8,100	1,500	15,100	13,400	(1,700)
Bad debts	11,600	10,700	(900)	57,700	80,700	23,000
Postage	18,700	20,400	1,700	131,400	70,900	(60,500)
Contributions	47,900	47,500	(400)	316,800	212,300	(104,500)
Sundry	42,100	34,900	(7,200)	232,700	331,900	99,200
TOTAL	$660,100	$691,600	$31,500	$3,826,100	$3,606,300	($219,800)

Financial Comparison Analysis

Disk File Name

FIN_07.XLS

Using This Form

Use this form to compare your company to the average firm in your industry. The financial comparison analyses is a diagnostic tool that will help you to pinpoint previously unnoticed strengths and weaknesses. This form is best used in the worksheet.

Entering Data

Enter all data into the unprotected cells provided. The first year [1] is unprotected and determines the subsequent years of the analysis. Totals, shareholders' equity, and financial ratios are all calculated automatically.

Printing This Form

Click the printer tool in the toolbar or choose Print from the File menu.

Adapting This Form

You could also use this form to compare the results of an independent corporate division with the results of the parent corporation in order to measure the differences in financial performance.

Financial Comparison Analysis
Rabbett-Dado Manufacturing, Inc.

❶

	Industry Average			Company Actual		
	1989	1990	1991	1989	1990	1991
ASSETS						
Cash	$1,500	$1,560	$1,490	$2,230	$2,450	$2,670
Accounts receivable	250	300	360	370	420	440
Inventory	500	650	740	800	875	840
Total Current Assets	2,250	2,510	2,590	3,400	3,745	3,950
Fixed assets (net)	1,250	1,340	1,290	2,650	2,790	2,850
TOTAL ASSETS	$3,500	$3,850	$3,880	$6,050	$6,535	$6,800
LIABILITIES & EQUITY						
Accts & notes payable	$1,800	$1,870	$1,910	$3,370	$3,650	$3,975
Accrued & other payables	350	380	385	590	635	650
Total Current Liabilities	2,150	2,250	2,295	3,960	4,285	4,625
Long-term debt	800	940	1,060	1,650	1,780	1,825
Total Debt	2,950	3,190	3,355	5,610	6,065	6,450
Shareholders' equity	550	660	525	440	470	350
TOTAL LIABILITIES & EQUITY	$3,500	$3,850	$3,880	$6,050	$6,535	$6,800
INCOME DATA						
Net sales	$1,900	$2,250	$1,985	$3,540	$3,740	$3,850
Cost of goods sold	1,095	1,250	1,125	1,830	1,910	2,250
Gross Profit	805	1,000	860	1,710	1,830	1,600
Operating expenses	250	420	365	780	830	790
Operating profit	555	580	495	930	1,000	810
All other expenses (net)	375	410	420	640	705	750
PROFIT BEFORE TAXES	$180	$170	$75	$290	$295	$60
FINANCIAL RATIOS						
Current	1.0	1.1	1.1	0.9	0.9	0.9
Total debt / total assets	0.8	0.8	0.9	0.9	0.9	0.9
Total debt / equity	5.4	4.8	6.4	12.8	12.9	18.4
Collection period days	48.0	48.7	66.2	38.1	41.0	41.7
Net sales / inventory	3.8	3.5	2.7	4.4	4.3	4.6
Total assets turnover	0.5	0.6	0.5	0.6	0.6	0.6
Gross profit margin	42%	44%	43%	48%	49%	42%
Operating profit margin	29%	26%	25%	26%	27%	21%
Return on equity	33%	26%	14%	66%	63%	17%

Monthly Cash-Flow Budget

Disk File Name

FIN_08.XLS

Using This Form

Use this form to plan your business's cash flow. It provides data entry areas for cash inflows and outflows from both operations and financing. The form can be filled out either on paper or electronically.

Entering Data

Enter data into the unprotected cells. The beginning cash balance [1] is entered in the first month and calculated for all subsequent months. Note that the total column summarizes the entire year [2], from the first month's beginning balance to the last month's ending balance. Change the starting month by typing the first three letters of the month in cell B26 [3](for example Jan). The other months will be calculated automatically by formulas.

Printing This Form

Click the printer tool in the toolbar or choose Print from the File menu.

Cash Flow Budget

For January through December 1993

③ ② ①

	Jan	Feb	Mar	Apr	May	Jun	Jul	Aug	Sep	Oct	Nov	Dec	Total
Beginning cash balance	$1,450	$1,406	$1,487	$1,444	$1,507	$1,636	$1,554	$1,425	$1,492	$1,425	$1,518	$1,614	$1,450
Cash from operations	125	218	168	219	347	252	155	236	153	246	346	131	2,596
Total Available Cash	$1,575	$1,668	$1,618	$1,669	$1,797	$1,702	$1,605	$1,686	$1,603	$1,696	$1,796	$1,581	$4,046
Less:													
Capital expenditures	$113	$123	$113	$106	$102	$94	$114	$126	$133	$126	$119	$123	$1,392
Interest	20	26	24	25	21	22	27	29	20	27	23	29	293
Dividends	2	4	3	5	0	2	1	2	3	2	4	5	33
Debt retirement	50	31	40	32	48	39	46	41	34	30	40	42	473
Other	0	0	0	0	0	0	0	0	0	2	0	0	2
Total Disbursements	$185	$184	$180	$168	$171	$157	$188	$198	$190	$187	$186	$199	$2,193
Cash Balance (Deficit)	$1,390	$1,484	$1,438	$1,501	$1,626	$1,545	$1,417	$1,488	$1,413	$1,509	$1,610	$1,382	$1,853
Add:													
Short-term loans	$6	$3	$6	$6	$10	$9	$8	$4	$7	$9	$4	$5	$77
Long-term loans	10	0	0	0	0	0	0	0	5	0	0	0	15
Capital stock issues	0	0	0	0	0	0	0	0	0	0	0	0	
Total Additions	$16	$3	$6	$6	$10	$9	$8	$4	$12	$9	$4	$5	$92
Ending Cash Balance	$1,406	$1,487	$1,444	$1,507	$1,636	$1,554	$1,425	$1,492	$1,425	$1,518	$1,614	$1,387	$1,945

Quarterly Cash-Flow Projection

Disk File Name

FIN_09.XLS

Using This Form

If happiness is a positive cash flow, this form will help foretell your short term happiness. It covers many, but not all, of the categories that affect the cash flow in most businesses. All of the row labels [1] are unprotected so that you can modify them with your own cash requirement categories.

Entering Data

Enter estimated [2] and actual [3] financial data into the appropriate columns for each month in the projection. The percentages each amount represents are calculated. Enter the starting month of the projection in cell C19. You can use this form even if you do not provide cash flow estimates; the estimates are included for your benefit to project future cash flows and identify cash problems in advance.

Printing This Form

Click the printer tool in the toolbar or choose Print from the File menu.

The Flimber Company

QUARTERLY CASH FLOW PROJECTION

PREPARED BY: Tyler Jones   DATE PREPARED: _____

	JANUARY				FEBRUARY				MARCH			
	ESTIMATE		ACTUAL		ESTIMATE		ACTUAL		ESTIMATE		ACTUAL	
CASH RECEIVED	$	% TOT	$	% TOT	$	% TOT	$	% TOT	$	% TOT	$	% TOT
Cash on Hand, 1st of Mo.	52,552	28%	54,530	27%	39,689	100%	53,061	100%	39,689	100%	53,061	100%
Cash Receipts Total	56,524	30%	61,202	30%		0%		0%		0%		0%
Cash Sales	3,821	2%	5,485	3%		0%		0%		0%		0%
Collections	59,014	32%	61,001	30%		0%		0%		0%		0%
Loans	15,121	8%	18,452	9%		0%		0%		0%		0%
TOTAL CASH AVAILABLE	187,032		200,670		39,689		53,061		39,689		53,061	
CASH DISBURSED												
Salaries and Wages	14,752	12%	15,855	13%								
Payroll Taxes	2,909	2%	3,102	3%								
Rent/Mortgage	1,659	1%	1,659	1%								
Health Insurance	1,041	1%	1,085	1%								
Business Insurance	14,871	12%	12,885	11%								
Office Supplies	5,404	4%	3,505	3%								
Utilities	7,316	6%	7,105	6%								
Telephone	4,790	4%	5,588	5%								
Repairs and Maintenance	4,378	4%	4,155	3%								
Operating Supplies	2,805	2%	3,950	3%								
Taxes, Licenses	2,800	2%	3,200	3%								
Professional Fees	3,437	3%	1,575	1%								
Commissions	13,716	11%	15,850	13%								
Travel	3,734	3%	4,580	4%								
Entertainment	6,806	6%	6,128	5%								
Purchases	4,140	3%	4,500	4%								
Advertising	1,957	2%	2,850	2%								
Transportation	14,776	12%	13,505	11%								
Other	12,352	10%	11,318	9%								
TOTAL DISBURSEMENT	123,643		122,395									
CASH POSITION												
Loan Payment w/ Interest	8,214	6%	8,214	6%								
Capital Purchases	2,080	1%	1,500	1%								
Owner's Withdrawal	13,406	9%	15,500	11%								
TOTAL CASH PAID OUT	147,343		147,609									
END OF MONTH	39,689		53,061		39,689		53,061		39,689		53,061	

Project Cost Summary

Disk File Name

FIN_10.XLS

Using This Form

Before undertaking a major project, use this form to analyze its financial terms, and to track its performance after it is approved. The form calls for calculating a set of financial evaluations that are not included in the file, but that you can find in most standard financial management texts. The projected numbers [1], which are usually entered as annual values, are included so that you can compare the estimates with actuals; both the projected and actual numbers can be entered without the other numbers.

Entering Data

You may enter data on the worksheet itself. You can use Text Edit to enter the Project Description and Project Justification. The various analyses [2] in rows 57 to 58 are intended to be entered as values.

Printing This Form

Click the printer tool in the toolbar or choose Print from the File menu.

Project Cost Summary

APPROPRIATION DETAIL

Project Title
Flange Finishing Machine
Project Number
M-00908

Plant Mgr
M. T. Pokkets
Responsibility Center #
Machine Shop

Product Lines
S,T,R
Purpose of Request

Cost Distribution
Elsewhere
Completion date
Nov 1993

PROJECT DESCRIPTION

We have to replace the old flange finishers soon. Frimple Inc. is looking for a test site for the 5000 series of flange finishers.

PROJECT JUSTIFICATION

The Frimple 5000 flange finishers create less burring and make it easier to design the molds with shorter sprues. It'll also reduce flashing. That should make it possible for us to use more re-processed materials and cut costs even further.

INVESTMENT SUMMARY

❶

		PROJECTED by YEAR						ACTUAL by YEAR			
	START UP	1	2	3	4	5	START UP	1	2	3	4	5
Capital Investment	75,152	5,200					125,852					
Working Capital		35,000	31,000	22,000	14,000	13,000						
Total Investment	75,152	40,200	31,000	22,000	14,000	13,000	125,852					
Sales		52,000	65,000	82,000	88,000	91,000						
Net Income		31,000	45,000	68,000	71,000	82,000						
Cash Flow		(9,200)	14,000	46,000	57,000	69,000	(125,852)					
Cum. Cash Flow		(9,200)	14,000	46,000	57,000	69,000	(125,852)					

ANALYSIS

❷

Discounted Return on Investment	15.20%	Internal Rate of Return	13.75%
Profitability Index	1.2	Modified Internal Rate of Return	10.90%
		Payback in Years	3.5
		Discounted Payback	4.2

APPROVALS

Prepared By _____ SIGNATURE   **VP Finance**

VP Responsible _____ SIGNATURE   **President** _____ SIGNATURE

Date 8/15/93   **Date** _____   _____ SIGNATURE

Commercial Credit Application

Disk File Name

FIN_11.XLS

Using This Form

Use this form if your business wishes to grant credit to other businesses or individuals. This form is intended to be filled out on paper by businesses or individuals.

Entering Data

You may customize the form by filling in your company's name, address, credit manager [1], and telephone number in the unprotected cells provided. The remainder of the form would ordinarily be filled out on paper.

Printing This Form

Click the printer tool in the toolbar or choose Print from the File menu.

Commercial Credit Application

	T	Name	Amazing Grates, Inc.	F	Name	Culverts "R" Us
	O	Address	10500 Lackman Road	R	Address	164 Old Elm Street
		City/State/Zip	Sam Hill, NH 03875	O	City/State/Zip	Pleasant Valley, MA 02001
		Credit Mgr	Reggie Stree ❶	M		
		Phone	(603) 555-1212		Phone	(508) 555-1212

Business Type: ☐ Sole Proprietor ☐ Partnership ☒ Corporation: State of Massachusetts

How long in business: 2 years   D&B Number: 44789-2348902-54893

Names/Addresses of Individuals or Partners   -or-   Name/Title/Phone Number of Corporate Officers

Annette Profitt, President and CEO, (508) 555-1212, ext. 123

Lois Price, VP and CFO, (508) 555-1212, ext. 456

Dot U. Rize, VP and Corporate Counsel, (508) 555-1212, ext. 789

Name of Person to Contact Regarding Purchase Orders and Invoices, Title, Address, and Phone Number

Paul Treesome, Accounts Payable Clerk, (508) 555-1212, ext. 321

Ida Claire, Import/Export Manager, (800) 555-1212, ext. 654

Bank Reference	Account Number, Contact, Title, and Phone Number
WayBank, Old Country Store Branch	Account # 60609-10023-V7R3A8
1364 Chaucer Row	Lottie Dah, Corporate Account Representative
Pleasant Valley, MA 02001	(508) 555-2121, ext. 987

Trade References: Company Name, Address, Contact and Title, and Phone Number

Goliath Temporaries, Inc., Gath, SD, Phyllis Stein, Contracts (605) 555-1212

Stationary Stationery, Inc., Newburgh, NY, Beau Thai, Customer Relations (212) 976-1000

The above information is submitted for the sole purpose of opening an account and I hereby certify the information to be true.	SIGNED Steve A. Door
	TITLE Foreman
	DATE November 19, 1992

Credit History

Disk File Name

FIN_12.XLS

Using This Form

This form is used by businesses to track the credit history of their customers. Because it uses no calculations, the form can be used almost as effectively on paper as electronically.

Entering Data

Enter data into unprotected cells. The cells in the date column [1] use the mm/dd/yy format. These cells accept text (for example, May 15, 1993) or date numbers (such as those using the DATE function).

Printing This Form

Click the printer tool in the toolbar or choose Print from the File menu.

CREDIT HISTORY

Name Chuck S. N. DeMayle   Spouse Sen Mi

Address 49 Terrystone Walk

North Columbia, KS 66430

Phone (913) 555-1212

Bus. Name Hi-Tech Household Help   Bus. Name

Address 49 Terrystone Walk   Bus. Address

North Columbia, KS 66430

Bus. Phone (913) 555-1212   Bus. Phone

❶

Date Approved	Credit Line	Payment Due Amount	Payment Due Date	Payment Received Amount	Payment Received Date	Balance	Date of 1st Notice	Date of 2d Notice
03/15/91	$5,000	115.00	07/21/92	1,000.00	07/14/92	1,248.04		

Phone Call _____   Date Sent to Attorney _____

Disposition _____

Credit Control List

Disk File Name

FIN_13.XLS

Using This Form

This form is used to track customers to whom credit has been granted. Information recorded includes the account number, account name, date opened, and details of the credit line and payment history. Like other Winning Forms, the Credit Control List can be used on paper.

Entering Data

Enter data into unprotected cells. All cells in the Date Opened column and cells H21 and J21 [1] use the mm/dd/yy format, so they will accept dates either as values or with the DATE function. Note that the Credit Available [2] and the Credit Used [3] columns are calculated from the Credit Line and Outstanding Balance columns.

Printing This Form

Click the printer tool in the toolbar or choose Print from the File menu.

Adapting This Form

Once you have entered information into this form, you can perform some Excel functions to analyze your data. For instance, you might want to sort your records by the credit available column to judge which accounts might be able to take advantage of certain promotions. Similarly, you might find it helpful to sort the records by the amount of money that is more than ninety days overdue. To learn more about sorting records in Excel, consult your Excel manual. If you want to create a second page of this report, transfer the Totals line of the first page to the top row of the new page and refer to the account name as *Previous Page Totals.*

CREDIT CONTROL LIST

Period from 02/01/92 ❶ to 06/30/92

Account #	Account Name	Date Opened	Credit Line	❷ Credit Available	❸ Credit Used	Current	30 days	60 days	90+ days
AB3410	The Garden Shop and Emporium	07/07/90	$14,000	$9,500	$4,500	$3,000	$1,500		
JF1903	Jambalaya Herbs and Spices	08/04/91	20,000	12,500	7,500	7,500			
	TOTALS		$34,000	$22,000	$12,000	$10,500	$1,500	$0	$0

Accounts Receivable Aging

Disk File Name

FIN_14.XLS

Using This Form

This form permits a company's current and past-due accounts receivable to be organized according to how long they have been outstanding. This form can be used either on paper or electronically.

Entering Data

Enter data into unprotected cells. Because many businesses maintain their accounts receivable in a database, you may wish to use file-linking formulas to reference the appropriate figures from another file. The cells in the column B [1] use the mm/dd/yy format. These cells accept text, such as Dec 15, or date numbers, such as DATE(92, 12,15) or DATEVALUE("12/15/92").

Printing This Form

Click the printer tool in the toolbar or choose Print from the File menu.

Accounts Receivable Aging
December 1993

CUSTOMER	Last Payment Date	Amount	Current 0-30	31-60	61-90	Past Due 91-119	120-150	150+	Total Due
Runyan Radiators, Inc.	09/12/93	$6,200		$2,140	$2,450		$2,880		$7,470
SteelCrate Container Corp.	10/07/93	5,300		1,010	1,300	2,140			4,450
Lab Planning Associates	10/23/93	7,600	950	2,790		1,310			5,050
Mimesis Systems, Inc.	12/03/93	4,600	2,840		1,160				4,000
TOTALS			$3,790	$5,940	$4,910	$3,450	$2,880		$20,970

❶

Overdue Account File

Disk File Name

FIN_15.XLS

Using This Form

Use this form to help manage your collection efforts. For each over-due account, the address, employer, guarantor, current account status, and collection history are listed. There are no formulas in this form, so it can be used quite effectively on paper.

Entering Data

Enter data into unprotected cells. Enter dates either as values or with the DATE function [1]. The date columns use the mm/dd/yy format.

Printing This Form

Click the printer tool in the toolbar or choose Print from the File menu.

OVERDUE ACCOUNT FILE

Name Yuri Pulsive   Phone (919) 555-2121

Address 8192 Column Row, Apt. A1

Frankston, NC 27410

Employer Medical News Network, Inc.   Phone (919) 555-1212

Address 575 Technology Square

Chapel Hill, NC 27512

Guarantor _____   Phone _____

Address _____

_____

❶

Date	Amount Paid	Balance Due
11/15/92	350.00	510.82
12/29/92	100.00	423.63
03/20/93	50.00	398.21

Date	Amount Paid	Balance Due

Date	History of Collection Efforts
11/01/92	First Warning Letter
03/12/93	Level 3 Dunning letter: placed on cash-only basis

Invoice

Disk File Name

FIN_16.XLS

Using This Form

All cash flow starts with an invoice. This invoice form is one of the most basic you can find.

Entering Data

Enter all dates as values [1]. If you take more than one line for a description, make sure you enter the quantity [2] and price on the same row, or you may get an incorrect answer. The cell where tax is entered [3] is unprotected so that you can enter any tax as a value, or enter a formula that calculates a tax, as your state requires.

Printing This Form

Click the printer tool in the toolbar or choose Print from the File menu.

The FLIMBER Company

The Finest in Flanges and Brackets

Lorain, OH 09090   (987) 878-9909

INVOICE

SOLD TO

Flotsam Foundries, Ltd
909 Happler Highway
Hillside NY 98765

SHIPPED TO

Same

INVOICE NUMBER	09-987-11
INVOICE DATE	5/5/92 ❶
OUR ORDER NO.	909-QT2
YOUR ORDER NO.	NN-090909
TERMS	Net 30
SALESMAN	MT Ouellette
SHIPPED VIA	Air
F.O.B.	Lorain, OH
PPD. or COLL.	COLL

QUANTITY	DESCRIPTION	PRICE	AMOUNT
❷ 2,522	Reconditioned Flotsam Flailing Motors (45 amp 321 v no resistors)	47.58	119,996.76
13,522	Electric Hash Thrashers (45 knife, 2mm particle)	5.91	79,915.02
	SUBTOTAL		199,911.78
	TAX		❸
	FREIGHT		
			$199,911.78 PAY THIS AMOUNT

If you have any questions about this invoice call:
Sally O'Connor   (999) 876-5555

MAKE CHECKS PAYABLE TO

The Flimber Company
Attn: Accounts Payable Department
1212 Elyria Highway
Lorain, OH 09090

THANK YOU FOR YOUR BUSINESS!

Service Invoice

Disk File Name

FIN_17.XLS

Using This Form

Use this invoice form to document the use of parts performance of services. Note that this invoice can use a sales tax on parts and labor. If you collect a tax only on parts *or* services (or on neither), enter zeros (0) in cell C19 or E19 (or both).

Entering Data

The form can be printed and filled out by hand, or it can be filled out in the worksheet. Enter dates as values or with the DATE function [1]. Enter the invoice number in cell A35 [2].

Printing This Form

Click the printer tool in the toolbar or choose Print from the File menu.

Ferd Berfle's Fazzle Blat Repair

RFD 09 COD
South Upper Crabtree PA

Service Invoice

SOLD TO	SERVICED AT
Sid's Incessant Talking Machines 45 Sixth St Gabby Heights PA 09090	Same

INVOICE NUMBER	MAKE OF EQUIPMENT	MODEL #	SERIAL #	DATE REPAIRED
92-098 ❷	Blister Mfg	876	0101010	11/14/92

PARTS USED

QTY	DESCRIPTION	PRICE	AMOUNT
1	Feezil fratz (unswitched)	18.76	18.76
8	Little pink plugs (grounded)	4.32	34.56

SERVICE PERSON	DATE	HOURS	RATE/HR	AMOUNT		
Charley Hoarce	5/6/92 ❶	12.0	$40.00	$480.00	Parts	$53.32
Horace Charles	5/7/92	4.0	65.00	$260.00	Labor	740.00
					Tax	69.27
					TOTAL	$862.59
					GUARANTEED FOR 30 DAYS	
					AGAINST FAULTY LABOR	
			TOTAL	$740.00	AND MATERIALS ONLY	

COMMENTS:
We thought you'd like the little pink plugs in your 18 wheeler, so we put them in for you.

Come by next month for our fuzzy dice special.

_____ _____
SERVICE SUPERVISED BY   SIGNED

Auto Expense Report

Disk File Name

FIN_18.XLS

Using This Form

Use this form to keep a record of your business-related auto expenses. This form may be used on paper or in the worksheet.

Entering Data

Enter data into the unprotected cells. Enter a date in cell B30 [1]. Be sure to use a date format that Excel recognizes. If you are not reimbursed for expenses, you can clear the signature section [2] at the bottom of the form. The mileage reimbursement rate is entered in cell E19 (not shown in the illustration).

Printing This Form

Click the printer tool in the toolbar or choose Print from the File menu.

KMT Software, Inc.
PLUG AND PLAY PRODUCTIVITY
190 Old Derby Street
Hingham, MA 02043

Auto Expense Report

EMPLOYEE _____
SALES OFFICE _____
ADDRESS _____
CITY _____
STATE _____   ZIP _____

WEEK ENDING ❶
11/21/92

TERRITORY NO.	BRANCH/REGION OR ZONE	PRODUCT LINE/SALES GROUP	COMPANY CHARGE CARD NO.

DATE	ODOMETER READING START	ODOMETER READING STOP	MILEAGE	REIMBURSED @ 22 CENTS PER MILE	GAS OIL	PARKING/ TOLLS	REPAIR MAINT	PAYMENT METHOD COMPANY CHARGE	PAYMENT METHOD EMPLOYEE CHARGE	PAYMENT METHOD CASH	DAILY TOTALS
11/15/92	13,775	13,781	6	1.32	18.00	4.50	16.00	16.00	18.00	5.82	39.82
11/16/92	13,781	13,804	23	5.06						5.06	5.06
11/17/92	13,804					8.50	28.00			36.50	36.50
11/18/92	13,804	13,877	73	16.06	5.00	7.00				28.06	28.06
11/19/92	13,877						352.00	352.00		0.00	352.00
11/20/92	13,877	14,210	333	73.26	12.00					85.26	85.26
11/21/92	14,210										
TOTALS			435	95.70	35.00	20.00	396.00	368.00	18.00	160.70	546.70

SIGNATURES ❷

PREPARER / TITLE _____   DATE _____

APPROVED BY / TITLE _____   DATE _____

MONTHLY AUTO EXPENSES	
LESS CASH ADVANCE	25.00
LESS CHARGES TO COMPANY	368.00
BALANCE DUE COMPANY	0.00
BALANCE DUE EMPLOYEE	153.70

Auto Expense Report 2

Disk File Name

FIN_19.XLS

Using This Form

Use this form to keep a record of your business-related auto expenses. If you are not reimbursed for expenses, you can erase the signature section [1]. Note that this form does not provide for mileage reimbursement. Employees who drive company cars will find this form helpful to claim reimbursable expenses connected with gas, tolls, and automobile maintenance. A self-employed businessperson can use the form to keep track of expenses for tax purposes.

Entering Data

Enter data into the appropriate unprotected cells in the form, or print the form and fill it in manually. If you want to fill in the dates manually, just erase cells C19 and F19. If you do not enter a year in cell F19, the form will assume the current year. The form automatically enters all of the expenses as cash payments, and automatically calculates the differences when you enter company charges and your charges.

Printing This Form

Click the printer tool in the toolbar or choose Print from the File menu.

Adapting This Form

If you are self-employed and you write off mileage expenses, you could easily add a formula at the bottom of the form to multiply cell D69 [2] by the reimbursable mileage rate (for example, D69*.27).

Flimber Brackets, Inc.

AUTO EXPENSE REPORT

190 Old Derby Street
Hingham MA 02043

MONTH ENDING   May 31, 1993

EMPLOYEE M. T. Ouellette	ADDRESS 55 Fifteenth Street	
SALES OFFICE Home Office	CITY Philadelphia	
	STATE MA	09090-0909
		ZIP

TERRITORY NO.	BRANCH/REGION OR ZONE	PRODUCT LINE/SALES GROUP	COMPANY CHARGE CARD NO.

DATE	ODOMETER READING START	ODOMETER READING STOP	MILEAGE	GAS & OIL	PARKING/ TOLLS	MISC.	COMPANY CHARGE	EMPLOYEE CHARGE	CASH	DAILY TOTALS
1-May	12,501			7.25					7.25	7.25
2-May	12,501	12,588	87	10.68					10.68	10.68
3-May	12,588				8.00				8.00	8.00
4-May	12,588	12,594	6	12.54					12.54	12.54
5-May	12,594	12,602	8	13.11		67.85			80.96	80.96
6-May	12,602	12,685	83							
7-May	12,685	12,811	126	13.57					13.57	13.57
8-May	12,811									
9-May	12,811									
10-May	12,811			5.34	2.00				7.34	7.34
11-May	12,811	12,828	17	15.34					15.34	15.34
12-May	12,828									
13-May	12,828									
14-May	12,828					185.95	185.95		0.00	185.95
15-May	12,828	12,912	84		1.00				1.00	1.00
16-May	12,912			10.78					10.78	10.78
17-May	12,912									
18-May	12,912	13,021	109		2.00				2.00	2.00
19-May	13,021			15.25					15.25	15.25
20-May	13,021									
21-May	13,021			20.80					20.80	20.80
22-May	13,021			13.51					13.51	13.51
23-May	13,021			13.86					13.86	13.86
24-May	13,021	13,055	34	15.50					15.50	15.50
25-May	13,055			13.04					13.04	13.04
26-May	13,055			7.64					7.64	7.64
27-May	13,055			13.61					13.61	13.61
28-May	13,055			14.98					14.98	14.98
29-May	13,055			12.89					12.89	12.89
30-May	13,055									
31-May	13,055									
		TOTALS	554	229.69	13.00	253.80	185.95		310.54	496.49

SUMMARY				BALANCE PAYABLE TO			
Cash Advance	125.00	Charge to Company	185.95	Company	0.00	Employee	185.54

PREPARER SIGNATURE / TITLE   DATE   APPROVAL SIGNATURE / TITLE   DATE

Expense Report

Disk File Name

FIN_20.XLS

Using This Form

This is a standard, but flexible, expense report form. You can change most of the items on it without unprotecting the worksheet. Meals are subtotaled separately to make tax calculations simpler at year end. You can enter additional expense categories in rows 45 through 47—the cells are unprotected. The entries will be calculated and totaled automatically.

Entering Data

Enter the ending date for the report in cell J24 [1] using the DATE function or as a value that Excel recognizes as a date. If you enter zero in E19, not shown in the figure, the mileage reimbursement line will be blank and you can use it for other purposes after erasing its calculations. This form automatically enters the days and dates of the seven-day period for which you wish to report expenses. Simply enter the last day of the week (or the last day of any seven-day period) as a value that Excel recognizes as a date or using the DATE function in cell J24. The form automatically enters the days and dates. Then enter the mileage reimbursement rate in cell E19, and the form will automatically calculate the reimbursement based on the mileage entered in the column.

Printing This Form

Click the printer tool in the toolbar or choose Print from the File menu.

Expense Report
The FLIMBER Company

NAME C DeSousa

PERIOD ENDING 6/12/93

	06/06/93 SUN	06/07/93 MON	06/08/93 TUE	06/09/93 WED	06/10/93 THU	06/11/93 FRI	06/12/93 SAT	TOTALS
MILES DRIVEN	145							145
REIMBURSEMENT	34.80							34.80
PARKING AND TOLLS								
AUTO RENTAL	12.50			25.00				37.50
TAXI / LIMO				1.25				1.25
OTHER (RAIL OR BUS)								
AIRFARE								
TRANSPORTATION TOTAL	47.30			26.25				73.55
LODGING	162.00			181.00			251.00	594.00
BREAKFAST	12.50	10.00		3.75	4.75			31.00
LUNCH	1.87							1.87
DINNER	18.65	23.00	18.25		19.75		15.00	94.65
SUB-TOTAL MEALS	33.02	33.00	18.25	3.75	24.50		15.00	127.52
TRAVEL & MEALS SUBTOTALS	195.02	33.00	18.25	184.75	24.50		266.00	721.52
SUPPLIES / EQUIPMENT								
PHONE, FAX		0.85	2.75					3.60
ENTERTAINMENT			1,000.00	187.75				1,187.75
TOTAL PER DAY	242.32	33.85	1,021.00	398.75	24.50		266.00	1,986.42

DETAILED ENTERTAINMENT RECORD

DATE	ITEM	PERSONS ENTERTAINED BUSINESS RELATIONSHIP	PLACE NAME & LOCATION	BUSINESS PURPOSE	AMOUNT
06/09/93	Dinner	Flo Chard, Bill Zardu - Custom	The Gravy Spot	Hash Sales	187.75

PURPOSE OF TRIP
Reconnoiter the territory

SUMMARY
TOTAL EXPENSES	1,986.42
LESS CASH ADVANCE	250.00
LESS COMPANY CHARGES	187.75
AMOUNT DUE EMPLOYEE	1,548.67
AMOUNT DUE COMPANY	0.00

PREPARED BY   DATE   APPROVED BY   DATE

Expense Report 2

Disk File Name

FIN_21.XLS

Using This Form

This form is laid out in landscape format with dates on its vertical axis of the form, rather than on the horizontal axis as in other expense reports. This expense report is intended to cover a seven-day period, and it automatically fills in the appropriate days when you enter the date of the end of the period. If the address is not necessary on every report, you can erase it. You may use that space, or the space next to it, to include information about the trip or the week's activities.

Entering Data

Enter the rate for reimbursing mileage in cell E19, then enter a date for the end of the reporting period in cell P25 [1], using either the DATE function or a value that Excel will recognize as a date. Enter all other data in the appropriate unprotected cells.

Printing This Form

Click the printer tool in the toolbar or choose Print from the File menu.

The FLIMBER Company

EXPENSE REPORT

ADDRESS LINE 1
ADDRESS LINE 2
CITY STATE ZIP

WEEK ENDING 7/5/92 ❶

EMPLOYEE Gunther K. Oelgeschlager   ADDRESS 123 Rodeo Drive
SALES OFFICE Oil City, PA   CITY Hollywood
TERRITORY Western PA   STATE PA   ZIP 657890
COMPANY CHARGE 5000-9876-9876-9999

DATE	AIR	TAXI/CAR RENTAL	GAS/OIL MAINT	MILES	RATE/MI 22 CTS	TOTAL TRANSP	HOTEL	BKFST	LUNCH	DINNER	ENTRTN	ALL OTHER	CHARGE TO CO	CHARGE TO EMPL	CASH	TOTALS
06/29	935.00			92	20.24	955.24	155.00	6.00	7.00	18.00			285.00		856.24	1,141.24
06/30				104	22.88	22.88	123.54	4.68	10.47	17.47					179.04	179.04
07/01				84	18.48	18.48	111.07	3.49	9.29	33.33					175.66	175.66
07/02				88	19.36	19.36	111.57	4.09	10.58	25.35					170.95	170.95
07/03				42	9.24	9.24	107.07	5.05	4.88	21.29					147.53	147.53
07/04				124	27.28	27.28	82.66	5.13	6.16	26.81					148.04	148.04
07/05				25	5.50	5.50	126.76	2.89	8.11	35.59					178.85	178.85
TOTAL	935.00			559	122.98	1,057.98	817.67	31.33	56.49	177.84			285.00		1,856.31	2,141.31

ENTERTAINMENT DETAIL (ATTACH SEPARATE SHEET IF NECESSARY)

DATE	PERSONS ENTERTAINED	BUSINESS CONDUCTED	AMT

SUMMARY

LESS CASH ADVANCE	250.00
LESS COMPANY CHARGES	285.00
AMOUNT DUE COMPANY	0.00
AMOUNT DUE EMPLOYEE	1,606.31

PREPARER SIGNATURE / TITLE DATE

APPROVAL SIGNATURE / TITLE DATE

Expense Report 3

Disk File Name

FIN_22.XLS

Using This Form

This form is similar to Expense Report 2, but prints in portrait mode. It also sets the dates based on the beginning of the expense reporting period, not the end.

Entering Data

Enter the date in cell I26; you can enter the month and day, and Excel will supply the current year. Enter the mileage reimbursement rate in G19. If you erase the date in I26, the form will use Sun. through Sat. for the days. Note that if you erase the mileage amount, no calculations will show.

Printing This Form

Click the printer tool in the toolbar or choose Print from the File menu.

The FLIMBER Company

EXPENSE REPORT

NAME _____Algeria Finnegan_____   PERIOD FROM 7/4/93

	07/04/93	07/05/93	07/06/93	07/07/93	07/08/93	07/09/93	07/10/93	
	SUN	MON	TUE	WED	THU	FRI	SAT	TOTALS
Personal Miles	128	82	69	89	105	130		603
Mileage Expense	33.28	21.32	17.94	23.14	27.30	33.80		156.78
Parking and Tolls	2.75	4.85	9.00	5.00	3.00	5.60		30.20
Auto Rental								
Taxi / Limo								
Other (Air, Rail, or Bus)			3.25					3.25
TOTALS	36.03	26.17	30.19	28.14	30.30	39.40		190.23
Lodging	89.27	97.15	57.28	87.54	59.41	54.56	68.43	513.64
Breakfast	18.39	24.37	14.00	16.86	13.02	15.43	23.76	125.83
Lunch	8.34	16.86	21.12	8.43	16.93	13.18	22.20	107.06
Dinner	22.53	10.21	16.82	22.09	18.10	15.89	20.00	125.64
Sub-total Meals	49.26	51.44	51.94	47.38	48.05	44.50	65.96	358.53
TOTALS	138.53	148.59	109.22	134.92	107.46	99.06	134.39	872.17
Supplies / Equipment	5.80	12.10	14.20	5.00	3.60	9.80	13.30	63.80
Phone, FAX	14.30	3.90	10.00	6.60	4.00	5.70	3.10	47.60
Entertainment (below)				62.00				62.00
TOTAL PER DAY	194.66	190.76	163.61	236.66	145.36	153.96	150.79	1,235.80

DETAILED ENTERTAINMENT RECORD

DATE	ITEM	PERSONS ENTERTAINED BUSINESS RELATIONSHIP	PLACE NAME LOCATION	BUSINESS PURPOSE	AMOUNT
7/7/93	Lunch	Damascus Q. Sweeney	Gravy Spot Cafe	Discuss Advertising Plans	62.00

PURPOSE OF TRIP

Sell, sell, sell!
Work the phones.

SUMMARY

TOTAL EXPENSES	1,235.80
LESS CASH ADVANCE	250.00
LESS COMPANY CHARGES	62.00
AMOUNT DUE EMPLOYEE	923.80
AMOUNT DUE COMPANY	0.00

PREPARED BY - SIGNATURE   DATE   APPROVED BY - SIGNATURE   DATE

Expense Budget

Disk File Name

FIN_23.XLS

Using This Form

Use this form to plan the personnel and operating expenses for a company or department. The form compares estimated and actual expenses, and may be filled out in two steps. Due to the numerous calculations, the form is best used electronically.

Entering Data

Enter the company or department name [1] and date [2] in the spaces provided. Then enter the remaining information into the unprotected cells. The form automatically calculates the dollar and percentage difference between estimated and actual figures.

Printing This Form

Click the printer tool in the toolbar or choose Print from the File menu.

Expense Budget

The Artful Dodger Corporation ❶
for April, 1993 ❷

		Estimate	Actual	Difference ($)	Difference (%)
PERSONNEL	Office	$25,000	$28,150	$3,150	12.6%
	Store	15,000	16,260	1,260	8.4%
	Salespeople	27,500	23,220	(4,280)	-15.6%
	Others	12,000	9,640	(2,360)	-19.7%
OPERATING	Advertising	$48,000	$37,260	($10,740)	-22.4%
	Bad Debts	4,000	6,130	2,130	53.3%
	Cash Discounts	6,000	9,260	3,260	54.3%
	Delivery Costs	3,400	5,150	1,750	51.5%
	Depreciation	3,000	2,570	(430)	-14.3%
	Dues and Subscriptions	500	370	(130)	-26.0%
	Employee Benefits	14,000	12,850	(1,150)	-8.2%
	Insurance	6,000	4,520	(1,480)	-24.7%
	Interest	450	440	(10)	-2.2%
	Legal and Auditing	1,000	1,300	300	30.0%
	Maintenance and Repairs	1,500	1,420	(80)	-5.3%
	Office Supplies	300	370	70	23.3%
	Postage	125	160	35	28.0%
	Rent or Mortgage	2,500	3,570	1,070	42.8%
	Sales Expenses	1,200	910	(290)	-24.2%
	Shipping and Storage	600	890	290	48.3%
	Supplies	250	200	(50)	-20.0%
	Taxes	2,000	1,320	(680)	-34.0%
	Telephone	250	260	10	4.0%
	Utilities	450	450	0	0.0%
	Other	2,000	2,460	460	23.0%
TOTAL EXPENSES		$177,025	$169,130	($7,895)	-4.5%

Daily Time Sheet

Disk File Name

FIN_24.XLS

Using This Form

Use this form to keep track of the time you spend on a job or at various tasks. The form contains the formulas necessary to calculate the elapsed time for each line item. This is an excellent form for professionals who track the time spent on various assignments and clients.

Entering Data

You may enter data directly into the worksheet or print a blank form and fill it out on-site.

Printing This Form

Click the printer tool in the toolbar or choose Print from the File menu.

Adapting This Form

This form could be adapted to monitor the start and finish of certain jobs; simply change the column headings to reflect the activities performed.

Law Offices of
Frantek, Mannick, and Wilde
555 Car Talk Plaza
Our Fair City MA 02020

DAILY TIME SHEET

NAME Huey Dewey, Jr.

DATE 5/2/92

Paralegal	Downtown
DEPARTMENT	LOCATION
09-888	121-48-0000
EMPLOYEE NUMBER	SOCIAL SECURITY NUMBER
NON-EXEMPT	
	PAYROLL CLASSIFICATION

TIME RECORD FOR

☐ Shift   ☒ Job   ☐ Contract _____

CONTRACT # / NAME

	CLIENT	PROFESSIONAL SERVICE	APPOINTMENT			TOTAL TIME	NEXT APPT
			Schedule	Start	Stop		
1	KMT, Inc.	Analyze Book Contract	8:30 AM	8:15 AM	10:00 AM	1:45	Fr 8:00 a
2	Mellin Enterprises	Close Office Bldg Sale	11:00 AM	11:00 AM	12:30 PM	1:30	NA
3	KMT, Inc.	Contract Analysis	NA	3:00 PM	4:30 PM	1:30	NA
4							
5							
6							
7							
8							
9							
10							
11							
12							
13							
14							
15							

REVIEW OF SERVICES RENDERED

2	# Apptmts	KMT, Inc.	Time 3 H 15 M
1	# Apptmts	Mellin	Time 1 H 30 M
	# Apptmts		Time
	# Apptmts		Time
	# Apptmts		Time
	# Apptmts		Time

SUPERVISOR _____ DATE

EMPLOYEE _____ DATE

PAYROLL _____ DATE

Purchases Log

Disk File Name

FIN_25.XLS

Using This Form

Use this form to record items you purchase, especially if you purchase them without a purchase order or out of petty cash. It will help you to find such important data as the date of purchase, if you should need such information for warranty purposes. You could use this form for your personal purchases by eliminating the PO # [1] and Category [2] columns and replacing them with the warranty number and the telephone number to call for support or service.

Entering Data

Enter data in the unprotected cells in the form, or print the form and fill it out manually.

Printing This Form

Click the printer tool in the toolbar or choose Print from the File menu.

AUNT BEA'S ATOMIC MUSTARD PLASTERS INC

P.O. BOX 969, ADFAF, PA 78431

② PURCHASES LOG ①

PAYMENT METHOD

DATE	PRODUCT	CATEGORY	REASON	VENDOR	PAID	CHECK	CASH	CREDIT	PO NUMBER
01/08/93	Winning Forms	Software	Admin	Egghead Software	19.95			19.95	Petty Cash
02/19/93	Enriched U-235	Fuel	Development	NRC	90,000.00			90,000.00	09-090908

CHAPTER
4

HUMAN RESOURCES FORMS

This section contains a series of forms to control and manage the hiring, interviewing, training, and dismissal of employees.

Request for Approval to Hire

Disk File Name

HUM_01.XLS

Using This Form

This form is used to tightly control the hiring process. It lists all the details of the candidate, the position, and the offer to be made. By capturing all of the details on one sheet of paper, misunderstandings can be minimized. This form can be used just as effectively on paper as in the worksheet.

Entering Data

Enter data into unprotected cells. Due to the narrow columns in this form, dates must be entered as values [1].

Printing This Form

Click the printer tool in the toolbar or choose Print from the File menu.

Request for Approval to Hire

❶

Requisition #   93-A1765   Date   February 18, 1993

Applicant   Kahn Telpitt

Job Title / Classification   Milling Machine Operator

(temporary replacement for Cy Attika on medical leave)

Part Time ☐   Full Time ☒   Permanent ☐   Temporary ☒

Replacement ☒   New Position ☐   Proposed Starting Salary $21.00 / hr

Reports to   Hank Raffted   Department   Fleet Maintenance

Description of Duties   Milling small repair parts, routine machine maintenance, genera

auto mechanics

Relocation Authorization   No relo necessary; applicant is local.

Policy Exceptions   None.

Start Date   March 8, 1993   Requested by   Denton Phender

NAME	TITLE	SIGNATURE	DATE
NAME	TITLE	SIGNATURE	DATE
NAME	TITLE	SIGNATURE	DATE

Interview Summary

Disk File Name

HUM_02.XLS

Using This Form

Use this form to help manage the interview process, bringing in the judgment of your peers, your boss, and selected subordinates as you interview potential candidates for employment. This form is intended to be used on paper, though it can be partially filled out electronically for the convenience of the interviewers.

Entering Data

Enter all data into unprotected cells.

Printing This Form

Click the printer tool in the toolbar or choose Print from the File menu.

Interview Summary

Applicant   Freda Livery

Position   Shipping Clerk   Date Interviewed   11 November 92

Date Available   Immediately   Salary Requested $12.50 an hour

EVALUATION	Good	Fair	Poor
Enthusiasm	X		
Experience		X	
Education	X		
Skills Required	X		
Attitude	X		
Appearance	X		
Other _____			
_____			
_____			

Comments

Freda can only work second shift due to her college schedule; she's available until June.

Her accounting training will be very helpful.

Recommendation

Review staff scheduling issues. If there's no problem, make an offer to start a week

from Monday.

INTERVIEWER SIGNATURE

New Employee Record Chart

Disk File Name

HUM_03.XLS

Using This Form

Use this form to see that you have all of the necessary records and information when bringing on a new employee. Included are standard items such as employment application and proof of citizenship or visa, as well as items specific to the position or to your company, such as trade secret agreement and security clearance. This form is intended to be filled out on paper, though you may want to complete the basic employee information electronically.

Entering Data

Enter all data into unprotected cells. Dates should be entered as values. The Other category at the bottom of the form contains lines for custom entries.

Printing This Form

Click the printer tool in the toolbar or choose Print from the File menu.

Adapting This Form

You may wish to adapt this form and use it for an activity that is suitable to a two-column comparison or checklist. Simply unprotect the worksheet and change the labels to suit your needs, and you will be able to easily create a new form.

New Employee Record Chart

Employee   Lou Slipps   Date   November 21, 1992

Department Telemarketing   Start Date November 23, 1992

Document	Required	Completed
Employment Application	x	x
Personal Data Sheet	x	x
Proof of Citizenship or Visa		x
Background Check	x	x
W4 Document	x	
State Tax Withholding	x	
Fidelity Bond		
Physical / Medical Report		
Employment Contract	x	x
Non-Competition Agreement	x	x
Trade Secret Agreement		
Conflict of Interest Declaration	x	x
Indemnity Agreement	x	x
Security Clearance		
Other:		
Verification of Receipt of Employee Handbook	x	

Signature of Supervisor _____

Employee Orientation Checklist

Disk File Name

HUM_04.XLS

Using This Form

Use this form to make sure that new employees are sufficiently oriented to the job function and to your company's way of doing business. Even the best managers don't have a perfect memory; this form ensures that nothing falls through the cracks. It is intended to be filled out on paper, though you may want to complete the basic employee information electronically.

Entering Data

Enter all data into unprotected cells. Dates should be entered as values [1]. The Other category at the bottom of the form [2] contains lines for custom entries.

Printing This Form

Click the printer tool in the toolbar or choose Print from the File menu.

Employee Orientation Checklist

Employee   Kenny Dewitt   Position   Technician

Department   Post-Sales Support   Start Date   February 15, 1993 ❶

Item	Reviewed
Department Function and Goals	x
Schedule of Hours	x
Coworker Introduction	x
Locker / Desk / Office	x
Supplies and Storage	x
Department Safety Procedures	x
Equipment and Tools	x
Record-Keeping Procedures	x
Job Training	x
Overtime Policy	x
Other: ❷	
Voice Mail Procedures	x
Electronic Mail Instructions	x

I acknowledge that the items checked have been reviewed with me and I understand them.

February 15, 1993

_____   _____
EMPLOYEE SIGNATURE   DATE

_____
SUPERVISOR SIGNATURE

Employee Self-Evaluation

Disk File Name

HUM_05.XLS

Using This Form

This form is filled out by employees in order to promote constructive discussion during the performance evaluation process. The form has no formulas, and can be used effectively on paper or in the worksheet.

Entering Data

Enter all data into unprotected cells. The date can be entered as a value or using the DATE function [1].

Printing This Form

Click the printer tool in the toolbar or choose Print from the File menu.

Adapting This Form

You could easily adapt this form and use it for a variety of questionnaires and evaluations. For example, a teacher could use it as a course evaluation form and a product manager could use it to test the key features of a product.

Employee Self-Evaluation

Employee   Clark Kent   Date   21-Dec-92

List objectives which were met or exceeded during the performance review period.

1. Prevented Earth from being destroyed by space aliens.
2. Averted 4 natural disasters.
3. De-escalated global thermonuclear conflict.
4. Flossed every day.

List objectives which were not met during the performance review period.

1. Lex Luthor still on the loose.
2.
3.
4.

List your key strengths.

1. Faster than a speeding bullet.
2. More powerful than a locomotive.
3. Able to leap tall buildings at a single bound.

List your performance areas that need further development.

1. Kryptonite invulnerability.
2. Finding suitable places to change.

List your key goals and objectives for the next performance review period.

1. Protect the world from evil.
2. Stand up for life, liberty, and the American Way.
3. Keep from being blown to bits, irradiated, or otherwise incapacitated.
4. Get married.

Employee Performance Review

Disk File Name

HUM_06.XLS

Using This Form

This form is used to provide some structure to the employee performance evaluation process. It provides checkboxes for key performance measures such as work consistency, initiative, and communication skills. It also includes spaces for the signatures of both the employee and the reviewer. This form is intended to be filled out on paper, although, like all Winning Forms, it can also be used electronically.

Entering Data

Enter data into unprotected cells. Due to the narrow columns in this form, dates must be entered as values [1].

Printing This Form

Click the printer tool in the toolbar or choose Print from the File menu.

Adapting This Form

You can adapt this form for a variety of uses where you can use the four-column comparison. For example, the basic form could be used to evaluate courses, seminars, product features, or the conditions of a property you might be interested in purchasing.

Employee Performance Review

Employee   Earl E. Ryser   Date   5 January 1993 ❶

Department Expediting   Last Review

Reviewer   Sue Pervizor   Date   8 January 1992

	Excellent	Good	Fair	Poor
Honesty	X			
Productivity		X		
Work Quality	X			
Technical Skills	X			
Work Consistency			X	
Enthusiasm	X			
Cooperation		X		
Attitude		X		
Initiative	X			
Working Relations		X		
Creativity		X		
Punctuality	X			
Attendance		X		
Dependability		X		
Communication Skills		X		
Other:				
	☐	☐	☐	☐
	☐	☐	☐	☐

Comments   If Earl would stop playing computer games in the morning, he would rate an
overall "excellent" review. A fine employee nevertheless.

_____   _____
SIGNATURE OF EMPLOYEE   SIGNATURE OF REVIEWER

Personnel Activity Report

Disk File Name

HUM_07.XLS

Using This Form

Use this form to report summary personnel statistics on a depart-
mental or companywide basis. Total and percentage calculations
make it advantageous to maintain the form in the worksheet. Nevertheless, like other Winning Forms, it can be used on paper.

Entering Data

Enter all data into the unprotected cells provided. Cell G27 [1] uses
the mm/dd/yy format. You can either enter the data as values or using the DATE function. The totals and the percentage of hires to
interviews are calculated automatically [2]. All other figures are entered into the form.

Printing This Form

Click the printer tool in the toolbar or choose Print from the File
menu.

Design Notes

The row titled *Turnover rate* contains no formula and is designed to
be filled in manually. If you wish to automate this calculation, you
could enter the following formula to calculate the monthly turnover
rate.

Personnel Activity Report

For Month of January, 1993

Prepared by   Diane Aross and Sue Preems   Date Prepared   02/14/93 ❶

	Salaried	Hourly	Part Time	Total
Number of employees at beginning	12	4	2	18
Number of employees at end	12	5	2	19
Number of positions still open	1	1	1	3
Number of applicants interviewed	4	6	0	10
Number of applicants hired	1	2	0	3
Percentage of hires to interviews	25%	33%		30% ❷
Number of employees terminated	0	1	0	1
Number of employees resigned	1	0	0	1
Number of openings at beginning	1	2	0	3
Total requisitions to be filled	1	1	1	3
Requisitions received	0	0	1	1
Requisitions filled	0	1	0	1
Requisitions unfilled	1	1	1	3
Turnover rate	13%	18%	15%	16%

Comments

Skill redeployment nearing completion.

Employee Change Record

Disk File Name

HUM_08.XLS

Using This Form

Use this form to record changes in an employee's status. The printed page would typically become part of the employee's file in the personnel records of the company. The form is intended to be filled out on paper.

Entering Data

Enter all data into unprotected cells. Dates may be entered either as values or with the DATE function [1]. Cell E29 uses the d-mmm-yy format (for example 30-Sep-92) for date display.

Printing This Form

Click the printer tool in the toolbar or choose Print from the File menu.

Employee Change Record

Employee Name per Company Records			Employee Number
First	Middle	Last	
Jess	B.	Gunn	S86P99Y007

New or Corrected Name			Effective Date
First	Middle	Last	
Jess	B.	Kuzz	30-Sep-92 ❶

Current Information	Description	Changed To
Sr. Investigator	Title	Inspector
DD720	Job Code	HD1440
14	Grade Level	18
$54,000	Salary	$62,000
	Department	
	Supervisor	
	Status & Shift	
	Hours per Week	
	Performance Rating	
	Date of Last Increase	
	% Change	
	Number of Months	
	Annualized % Change	
	LOA Start Date	
	LOA End Date	
	Vacation Carryover	
	Other:	

Reason for Change
Jessica was promoted.
Records also updated to reflect new last name.

Approvals		
Supervisor		Supervisor
One-Over		One-Over
Human Resources		Human Resources

Employee Time Sheet

Disk File Name

HUM_09.XLS

Using This Form

This form tracks an employee's time, from the beginning to the end of the day, accounting for meals. This form can be used on paper or in the worksheet.

Entering Data

Enter all text, times, and dates into the unprotected cells provided. Dates may be entered using the DATE function or as values [1]. All date cells use the d-mmm-yy format (that is, 19-Feb-93) [2]. Note that the form does not calculate the number of hours worked [3], in order to give you flexibility in calculating overtime hours. Enter the hours as values, as they are totaled at the bottom of the form.

Printing This Form

Click the printer tool in the toolbar or choose Print from the File menu.

Employee Time Sheet

❶

Employee   Pam D. Monium   Pay Period Ending   19-Feb-93

Department Receiving

Date	Start Time	Meal Time	End Time	Regular Hrs	Overtime Hrs
❷ 08-Feb-93	8:15AM	12:30 to 1:00	5:30PM	❸ 8.75	0.00
09-Feb-93	8:00AM	12:00 to 12:30	6:00PM	9.50	0.00
10-Feb-93	8:00AM	12:30 to 1:00	6:00PM	9.50	0.00
11-Feb-93	7:30AM	11:30 to 12:00	6:30PM	10.50	0.00
12-Feb-93	8:30AM	12:30 to 1:00	5:00PM	1.75	6.25
15-Feb-93	8:00AM	12:00 to 12:30	6:00PM	9.50	0.00
16-Feb-93	7:30AM	11:30 to 12:00	6:30PM	10.50	0.00
17-Feb-93	8:00AM	12:30 to 1:00	6:30PM	10.00	0.00
18-Feb-93	8:15AM	12:30 to 1:00	5:45PM	9.00	0.00
19-Feb-93	8:30AM	12:30 to 1:30	5:00PM	1.00	6.50
20-Feb-93	8:00AM	NA	12:30PM	0.00	4.50
		Totals		80.00	17.25

_____

EMPLOYEE SIGNATURE

_____   22-Feb-93

SUPERVISOR SIGNATURE   DATE

Weekly Work Schedule

Disk File Name

HUM_10.XLS

Using This Form

Use this form to schedule up to twenty employees' work schedules for a week. The form can be used either electronically or on paper.

Entering Data

Enter all data into unprotected cells. The main body of the form is used to record the hours that each employee works. You can either enter the number of hours each person will work, or the start and end times. To insure that you fit all of the information in the cells, type A for AM and P for PM when entering the start and end times.

Printing This Form

Click the printer tool in the toolbar or choose Print from the File menu.

Weekly Work Schedule

Department Cafeteria

Week Ending 19 June 1993

Employee and Assignment	Sun	Mon	Tue	Wed	Thu	Fri	Sat
				Hours			
Corey Ander, Chef II		7	7	7	7	3	
Clem Chouder, Cashier		5	5	5	8	8	
Al Dontay, Short Order Cook		5	6	4	4	7	
Sue Keany, Baker	5	6	6	6	6	5	
Mara Nate, Salad Bar		4	3	3	3	3	
Emma Nemms, Snack Counter		7	7	7	7	7	
Andy Pasto, Short Order Cook		4	4	6	6	4	
George A. Peach, Cashier		8	8	8	5	3	
Hal O'Peenia, Chef		6	6	6	6	6	
Gus Potcho, Baker	5	4	4	4	4	7	
Hammond Swiss, Cashier		3	3	3	3	6	

Vacation Schedule

Disk File Name

HUM_11.XLS

Using This Form

This form allows a manager to chart employees' summer vacation time, so that scheduling conflicts can be identified and addressed. The form includes a space for each week of April through September.

Entering Data

Begin by entering the date (1 through 7) of the first Monday in April in cell D28 [1]. All the other dates (as well as the months) are determined by that number. Enter all remaining data in the unprotected cells provided. For each employee planning vacation time in April through September, enter an x [2] in the appropriate week, or shade the cell.

Printing This Form

Click the printer tool in the toolbar or choose Print from the File menu.

Vacation Schedule

YEAR: _____ 1993

DEPARTMENT: _____ Cafeteria

EMPLOYEE	Apr 5	12	19	26	May 3	10	17	24	31	Jun 7	14	21	28	Jul 5	12	19	26	Aug 2	9	16	23	30	Sep 6	13	20	27
Corey Ander	❶				X														X							
Al Burnin											❷X								X							
Clem Chouder														X						X						
Al Dontay								X				X	X													
Lynne Gweenie											X						X									
Sue Keany													X	X												
Mary Nate																				X	X					
Emma Nemms															X	X		X	X							
Andy Pasto												X									X					
George A. Peach															X			X								
Hal O'Peenia																X	X									
Gus Potcho										X																
Hammond Swiss																								X		

Receipt for Company Property

Disk File Name

HUM_12.XLS

Using This Form

Use this form to track company property checked out to employees. This form is intended to be used on paper, though it can also be used electronically.

Entering Data

Enter data into unprotected cells. The date entries can be made either as values or with the DATE function [1].

Printing This Form

Click the printer tool in the toolbar or choose Print from the File menu.

Receipt for Company Property

Employee   Anne T. Soshul

Department Accounting   Employee #   43762

    I acknowledge receipt of the company-owned equipment listed below. I agree to maintai the equipment in good condition and to return it when I cease working for the company, or earlier on request. I promise to report any loss or damage immediately. I further agree to us said property only for work-related purposes.

RECEIVED

Item	Qty	Serial #
MCR Adding Machine	1	JT9783-12

RETURNED

Returned to	Date
	########

_____
SIGNATURE

April 5, 1993   **❶**
DATE

Issued by _____

Employee Termination Checklist

Disk File Name

HUM_13.XLS

Using This Form

Use this form to insure that you complete all of the necessary actions when terminating an employee. Included are standard items such as return of desk and file keys and company documents, as well as items specific to the position or to your company, such as a confidentiality report. This form is intended to be filled out on paper, though you may want to complete the basic employee information electronically.

Entering Data

Enter all data into unprotected cells. Dates should be entered as values [1]. The Other category at the bottom of the form contains lines for custom entries.

Printing This Form

Click the printer tool in the toolbar or choose Print from the File menu.

Employee Termination Checklist

Employee   Wendy U. Leeve   Date   10-Jan-93 **❶**

Department Accounting

Each of the items below must be returned or completed
upon termination and before issuance of final pay check.

Return

Company Equipment	x
ID Badge	x
Company Credit Cards	x
Petty Cash Advances	NA
Expense Accounts	x
Desk and File Keys	x
Keys to Premises	x
Catalogs and Sales Materials	NA
Sample Products	x
Company Automobile	NA
Company Documents	x

Other:

Company Software	x
_____	

Complete

Exit Interview	NA
Expense Reports	x
Termination Form	x
Confidentiality Report	x
Benefits Review	x
Final Timesheet	x

Other:

Vacation Reconciliation	x
_____	

Comments   Due to return on 19-Jan to pick up remaining personal effects.

_____

_____

Signature of Supervisor   _____

CHAPTER

5

OPERATIONS FORMS

The forms in this section address your needs for inventory, production, materials control, and shipping forms. The section also contains forms for purchasing and quality control. Most are designed for internal use, though the purchase orders and bill-of-lading are external forms.

This section also contains an invaluable form for recording pertinent information about the PCs in your office.

Parts Inventory

Disk File Name

OPR_01.XLS

Using This Form

This form is designed to record the inventory of various parts in a given location. It can be used electronically or on paper.

Entering Data

Enter data for part numbers, quantities, and unit prices into the unprotected cells provided. The form contains calculations for extensions.

Printing This Form

Click the printer tool in the toolbar or choose Print from the File menu.

The FLIMBER Company

PARTS INVENTORY

Bin Number _____
Page _____
Of _____
Date _____

PART NUMBER	QTY	UNIT PRICE	EXTENSION	PART NUMBER	QTY	UNIT PRICE	EXTENSION
09-00934	234	1.75	409.50				
06-07771	1,600	3.26	5,216.00				
06-07680	522	6.70	3,497.40				
06-01052	1,620	1.09	1,765.80				
06-02544	1,143	6.48	7,406.64				
05-06149	543	4.06	2,204.58				
06-01421	578	3.04	1,757.12				
06-03944	100	2.94	294.00				
04-08563	986	6.68	6,586.48				
06-01043	732	3.24	2,371.68				
09-08131	1,635	7.29	11,919.15				
06-01775	1,241	6.98	8,662.18				
06-07923	1,560	4.44	6,926.40				
06-06744	1,228	3.58	4,396.24				
06-01905	1,735	5.07	8,796.45				
06-05345	1,667	4.50	7,501.50				
		SUB-TOTAL	$79,711.12			SUB-TOTAL	
						TOTAL	$79,711.12

Inventory

Disk File Name

OPR_02.XLS

Using This Form

Use this form both for taking and valuing the inventory in a given location. The form covers those cases in which several people work on different inventory tasks.

Entering Data

When you use the form for taking a physical inventory, enter data manually in the item [1], description [2], and unit columns [3]. Later, when you transcribe the manually entered data, you can add the unit price data [4] onto the worksheet, which will perform the extension calculation automatically.

Printing This Form

Click the printer tool in the toolbar or choose Print from the File menu.

INVENTORY

SHEET COMPLETED	
DATE	TRANSCRIBED BY
2/11/93	Mel Jones
TIME	TRANSCRIPT DATE
01:55 PM	2/15/93

DEPARTMENT		PRICED BY	DATE
Roanoke Warehouse - Store B		Bert Richter	
CALLED BY	DATE	EXTENDED BY	DATE
Harvey Teicher		Charlie Lieberfarb	
ENTERED BY	DATE	EXAMINED BY	DATE
Harry Rinaldi		Jerry Goldstein	

ITEM NO	DESCRIPTION	QTY	UNIT	UNIT PRICE	EXTENSION
	BALANCE CARRIED FORWARD				$135,852.51
UC-16403	Bow Satin - Red	186	Yards	3.39	630.54
SV-13189	Fireman Fred - Hose Reels	558	Pieces	1.03	574.74
EV-13895	Teddy Truck - Trailer Assembly	257	"	7.20	1,850.40
EV-16289	Teddy Truck - Cab Assembly	136	"	2.56	348.16
MR-14991	Big Bunny - Fuzzy Yellow	189	Pieces	17.82	3,367.98
	AMOUNT TO CARRY FORWARD				$142,624.33

Perpetual Inventory Control

Disk File Name

OPR_03.XLS

Using This Form

This form is designed to let you record the inventory status of a given part or item. Because there are relatively few formulas, this form can be used on paper as well as electronically.

Entering Data

You must enter data on every line of the form, especially in columns K [1] and F [2]; if you enter two zero values into these columns, the values in column L, the inventory balance [3], will be incorrect. Enter the sheet number in cell L26 [4]. The amount that should be carried forward to the next sheet and the next sheet number are at the bottom of the form (row 55). You may wish to use a file-linking formula in L30 [5] to link each successive sheet.

Printing This Form

Click the printer tool in the toolbar or choose Print from the File menu.

PERPETUAL INVENTORY CONTROL

ITEM	ITEM NUMBER	SHEET NUMBER
Flimber Bracket	0900993	2 ④

ORDERED				RECEIVED			DUE DATE	SOLD ①②③			BALANCE	COMMENTS
DATE	ORDER NO	VENDOR	QTY	DATE	QTY	BACKORDER		DATE	ORDER NO	QTY	BALANCE	COMMENTS
									BALANCE FORWARD ⑤		138	
06/17/91	H00987	Smith	103	07/04/91	103					75	166	
06/21/91	H00999	Beane	102	06/30/91	55	47				75	146	
06/25/91	H01003	Merrill	153	07/03/91	153						299	
06/30/91	H01007	Lynch	124	07/10/91	124					150	273	
07/03/91	H01009	Witter	164	07/13/91	164						437	
07/04/91		Reynolds		07/24/91						52	385	
07/07/91	H01015	Edwards	158	07/20/91	158					76	467	
07/13/91	H01019	Pierce	62	07/25/91	62					48	481	
07/16/91	H01022	Clayton	87	08/01/91	1						482	
07/23/91	H01025	Scott	171	08/02/91	171					123	530	
07/25/91		East		08/13/91	1					154	377	
07/30/91		Scott	167	08/12/91	167						544	
08/03/91		Scott		08/12/91	0					141	403	
08/08/91		Jones		08/16/91	12						415	
08/10/91		Gregory	36	08/23/91	36					46	405	
08/16/91		Clayton	107	09/02/91	107						512	
08/22/91		Clayton		09/03/91						14	498	
08/26/91		East		09/15/91						151	347	
09/01/91		Edwards	101	09/21/91	101						448	
09/02/91		Edwards		09/09/91						20	428	
09/08/91		Gregory	151	09/24/91	151					187	392	
09/13/91		Lake	107	09/22/91	107						499	
09/15/91		Lake		10/03/91						24	475	
10/22/91		Scott		11/03/91	0					14	461	
								CARRIED TO SHEET 3			461	

Production Reject Report

Disk File Name

OPR_04.XLS

Using This Form

Use this form to record the occurrence of and reasons for any rejects. If you have more than one production line, you may want to add a column for the production line on which the rejects occur. Similarly, you may want to use separate forms for different products.

Entering Data

This form is designed to be filled out by hand, though, like most Winning Forms, it can be filled out electronically. Enter all data into unprotected cells.

Printing This Form

Click the printer tool in the toolbar or choose Print from the File menu.

Adapting This Form

In a sense, this is a basic, six-column report form. You would have to remove protection, but any of the labels in the headings [1] can be changed. There are no formulas in the form, so you do not have to erase anything to create a new form.

Production Reject Report

REPORT DATE 12/18/92   **PERIOD OF ACTIVITY** 12/18/92 TO 2/10/93

PRODUCT NUMBER / NAME ❶	# OF ORDERS	OPEN ORDERS	% TOTAL PRODN	REJECT	REASON FOR REJECTS
Fuzzy Suits - Bunny Play Time	125	150	20.00%	20	Dirty Tails - Ripped Ears
Ladder Assemblies - Fire Fun	287	152	18.00%	14	Broken Slider Gear
Windshields - Drivin' Dan	1,851	2,104	2.50%	41	Cloudy Butyrate Mix - Regrind

Daily Production Report

Disk File Name

OPR_05.XLS

Using This Form

Use this form to track production activities in various parts of your operation, and to control scrap in the production process.

Entering Data

Enter data for the time in columns F, G, and H [1], [2], and [3], using labels. There are no time calculations in the worksheet. Enter weight data in columns I [4] and J [5]. Column K contains a calculation of scrap.

Printing This Form

Click the printer tool in the toolbar or choose Print from the File menu.

The *FLIMBER* Company

DAILY PRODUCTION REPORT

WORK CENTER | Jelly Jar Line
SHIFT | 7am-3pm
DATE | 11/5/92

SCHEDULE

PRODUCTION ORDER NUMBER	CUSTOMER	PRODUCT SIZE AND DESCRIPTION	ORDER QTY	① START	② STOP	③ HOURS	④ CHARGED WEIGHT	⑤ PRODUCT WEIGHT	SCRAP LOSS
JJ-005	Annie's Vermont Condiments	Funny Looking Jars	15,500	7:00 am	11:45 am	4:45 hrs	1365.8	1327.4	38.4
LL-9009	Aunt Bea's	7 oz Mustard Jars	54,000	10:00 am	11:55 pm	14 hrs	6750.0	6687.0	63.0

PRODUCTI

DELAYS

FROM	TO

EXPLANATION

PREPARED BY _____

APPROVED BY _____

Material Requisition

Disk File Name

OPR_06.XLS

Using This Form

The Material Requisition form is designed to let operating departments tell the purchasing department what they need, and when they need it. The purchasing department then places an order, and fills in the part of the form designed to record the actual costs and various other significant purchasing details. In effect, this form is the beginning of the purchasing cycle.

Entering Data

The form can be filled out manually or as a worksheet. The only calculations in the worksheet are in the extended price column [1].

Printing This Form

Click the printer tool in the toolbar or choose Print from the File menu.

The FLIMBER Company   MATERIAL REQUISITION

REQ DATE	REQUISITIONED BY	MUST HAVE BY	CHARGE TO ACCT.	DELIVER TO
2/6/93	Jim Nastix	2/28/93	Cost Center 90909	Roanoke Warehouse

ITEM	QTY	UNIT	DESCRIPTION	ESTIMATED COST	UNIT PRICE	EXTENDED
P-09	1,000	Pcs	Flimber Brackets	958.75	0.91	912.50
Q-45	767	lbs	Vinyl Records (scrap)	655.00	0.85	651.95

PURCHASING USE ONLY ❶

CERTIFICATION		SHIP VIA	APPROVED BY	DATE	TOTAL		TOTAL
YES	NO	P.I.E.	C. Lieberfarb	02/18	$1,613.75		$1,564.45

SUGGESTED VENDORS

1. KMT HARDWARE, INC (Elizabethport Facility)
2. FLANDERS FLIMBER BRACKETEERS
3.

PURCHASING USE ONLY

KMT no longer makes wooden flimber brackets -- according to Phil DeBochs. Phil is their new sales manager in charge of packaging. (note added by Slim Smith, 2/9/93)

VENDOR	VENDOR'S PROMISED SHIP DATE
FLANDERS	02/20/93

ADDRESS	RESALE	TAXABLE
Building 0909-8		
456 Industrial Lane	TERMS	P.O. NUMBER
CITY OF INDUSTRY, CA 99999-9876	Net 90	09-83284

CONTACT	TELEPHONE	BUYER	P.A. APPROVAL
Harry Rinaldi	(201)-555-9022	Ronald A. Mills	Carl Fabiano

Stock Balance Record

Disk File Name

OPR_07.XLS

Using This Form

Use this form to keep track of the use of a part or subassembly. The balance-on-hand calculation assumes that issuing an item is the same as using (or selling) it. The Used Month to Date column is included for comparisons. Document the source of information in the Reference column.

Entering Data

The calculations in this form depend on whether you enter a date into column A [1]. If you skip a date, your results may be incorrect, so make sure you enter a date into every row in column A. Enter all other data as text or values in the appropriate columns.

Printing This Form

Click the printer tool in the toolbar or choose Print from the File menu.

Stock Balance Record

ITEM Flimber Brackets

UNITS Pieces

LOCATION 2d Floor   SECTION C 15

EXPEDITE 500   REORDER 300

DATE ❶	REFERENCE	ISSUED	REC'D	ON ORDER	USED MO TO DATE	BALANCE
				OPENING BALANCE		55
12/12/91		85	455		425	425
12/16/91		44			469	381
12/30/91		35			504	346
01/01/92		56	100		56	390
01/03/92		81			137	309
01/05/92		21			158	288
01/09/92		41	125		199	372
01/14/92		52			251	320
01/21/92		21			272	299
01/26/92		35	180		307	444
01/26/92		56			363	388

Request for Quotation

Disk File Name

OPR_08.XLS

Using This Form

Use this form to request a bid from a vendor. When the quotations are returned, use a blank copy of this form for a quick summary. Consider sending each vendor two copies of the form: one for the vendor's response and one for filing.

Entering Data

This form can be prepared in the worksheet or filled out by hand. Enter data into unprotected cells.

Printing This Form

Click the printer tool in the toolbar or choose Print from the File menu.

FROM:

KMT Software, Inc.
190 Old Derby Street
Hingham, MA 02043
(617) 749-4779

Request for Quotation

TO:

| The Flimber Company |
| 55 Flimber Parkway |
| Totowhippaway NJ 09090 |

ADDRESS CORRESPONDENCE TO:

Jim Shortz
Seat Heater Division
299 Warm Way
Gotham MG 09090
PHONE   010-101-0101
FAX   99-999-0000

REQUEST DATE   8/22/93

This quotation number MUST appear on all QUOTATIONS and related CORRESPONDENCE.

QUOTATION NUMBER   990-009-88

DELIVERY REQUIRED BY	TERMS	DATE OF EARLIEST SHIPMENT
July 30, 1993	1 / 10; N / 30	8/15/93
REPLY REQUIRED BY	F.O.B.	SHIP VIA
June 15, 1993	Sandusky, OH	Overland

ITEM	QUANTITY	DESCRIPTION	UNIT PRICE	AMOUNT
	15,850	Blue Seat Heating Coils (IFG standard)	1.20	$19,020.00
			TOTAL	$19,020.00

SUMMARY	VENDOR 1	VENDOR 2	VENDOR 3	COMMENTS
QUANTITY	18,500			
ITEM				
TERMS	N 60			
F.O.B.	Lorain OH			
DELIVERY	PPd			

ORDER PLACED WITH _____   P.O. # _____

CIRCLE REASON

Lowest Price	Service	Other (explain below)
Quality	Only Source	_____
Best Delivery	Best Design	_____

Buyer _____   **Date** _____

Quotation Evaluation

Disk File Name

OPR_09.XLS

Using This Form

Use this form to record the details of competing bids for your business, and to analyze the unit cost. The form assumes that you will take any discount offered.

Entering Data

Enter data into the unprotected cells in the form, or print a blank form and fill it out by hand.

Printing This Form

Click the printer tool in the toolbar or choose Print from the File menu.

Adapting This Form

If you want to provide more space for text in the Remarks sections of the vendor evaluations, you can either increase the height (Format Set Row Height) of rows 34..35, and so on, or insert more rows (Edit Insert). Increasing the row height is probably the best bet if you are going to fill in the form manually, since you don't have to remove protection to do so, and will not have to reformat or erase any lines. If you do increase row height or insert additional rows, don't forget to reset the print area (Options Set Print Area).

Quotation Evaluation

DATE 9/9/92
JOB Printing WingThing Flyers
JOB NUMBER 88-99

DESCRIPTION 2 color marketing brochures
OF JOB for Winter sales campaign

	QTY	DELVRY SCHED	DISC TERMS	TOTAL PRICE	UNIT PRICE	DELIVERY CHARGE	NET PRICE	ADJ UNIT PRICE
FIRM The FLIMBER Co	15,000	10 days	7.00%	3,500.00	0.23	85.00	3,340.00	0.22
CONTACT Hugh Neekly								
PHONE 909-909-9090								
FAX 090-090-9876								

REMARKS Flimber may not be able to handle this job -- too small

	QTY	DELVRY SCHED	DISC TERMS	TOTAL PRICE	UNIT PRICE	DELIVERY CHARGE	NET PRICE	ADJ UNIT PRICE
FIRM Turandot Printing	15,000	1 week	3.00%	3,655.00	0.24	255.00	3,800.35	0.25
CONTACT								
PHONE								
FAX								

REMARKS This guy always answers in riddles . . . but he works all night if we need it.

FIRM
CONTACT
PHONE
FAX
REMARKS

FIRM
CONTACT
PHONE
FAX
REMARKS

FIRM
CONTACT
PHONE
FAX
REMARKS

COMMENTS

Quotation Record

Disk File Name

OPR_10.XLS

Using This Form

This form is used to keep a record of the quotations you receive from vendors, the details of each quote, and a quick evaluation of the vendor. The form also gives a cost per unit based on discounts and freight costs.

Entering Data

Enter dates [1] as values. You must enter values for the list price [2] and discounts [3], or the form will not generate a per-unit price.

Printing This Form

Click the printer tool in the toolbar or choose Print from the File menu.

Quotation Record

SPECIFICATION NO. 0090

MATERIAL NAME FLIMBER BRACKETS

UNIT PIECES

DESCRIPTION Annealed / anodized brackets for flimbers in the zattratch

COMMENTS

USAGE

PRODUCT	#	PRODUCT	#	PRODUCT	#
Mashers	1				
Thrashers	1				
Rippers	2				

① DATE	PURCHASE ORDER NO	QTY	② LIST PRICE	③ DISC	NET PRICE	FREIGHT	TOTAL COST	UNIT COST	VENDOR	REMARKS
09/03/92	A00000	100	1,555.00	15.00%	1,321.75	18.66	1,340.41	13.4041	Qubax, Inc	Good Delivery!
09/11/92	A00033	35	18.56	13.00%	16.15	1.25	17.40	0.4971	Sly Guys	Lots of rejects

Purchase Order

Disk File Name

OPR_11.XLS

Using This Form

Use this purchase order form just as you would a manual form. You can enter a multi-line description (double-space between items for readability), or you can enter up to twenty single-line entries.

Entering Data

You can enter dates [1] as values or using the DATE function. If you use a value, be sure that it is one of the formats that Excel recognizes as a date.

Printing This Form

Click the printer tool in the toolbar or choose Print from the File menu.

Adapting This Form

If the Unit column is unnecessary or if you want to remove it temporarily, remove protection (Options Unprotect Document) and erase cell B41 [2]. Then remove the line from B42..B58 using Format Border and clearing all selections. That will leave the Description heading off-center, so copy C41 [3] to B41 and erase C41. Finish by restoring protection (Options Protect Document). In effect, this procedure gives you an additional Purchase Order form.

The FLIMBER Company

70000 Uniform Road   Irregular, NX 76999   888-090-0101

PURCHASE ORDER

The following number must appear on all correspondence, acknowledgements, bills of lading, and invoices relating to this PO:

PURCHASE ORDER HI 009009

P O DATE	8/14/92 ❶
TERMS	Net 90
F.O.B.	Irregular, NX
SHIP VIA	

TO

Ben's Mountain Climbing Equipment
990 Umpteenth Lane
Millinocket ME, 09900

Attention: Phil N. D. Blank

ADDRESS CORRESPONDENCE TO

Name	Harry Rinaldi, Purchasing Mgr.
	The FLIMBER Company
	70000 Uniform Road
	Irregular, NX 76999
Phone	888-090-0101 Ext 999
FAX #	888-090-1999

QTY	UNIT	DESCRIPTION	UNIT PRICE	AMOUNT
12	GROSS	Magnesium Bagel Butterers with Retracting Blints	2.00	24.00
67	LBS	Cream Cheese	3.95	264.65
200			500.00	100,000.00
			subtotal	100,288.65

❷ (above UNIT column)   ❸ (above DESCRIPTION column)

PLEASE NOTIFY US IMMEDIATELY IF THIS	SHIPPING — PREPAID
ORDER CANNOT BE SHIPPED COMPLETE ON	TAX — 23.09
OR BEFORE 12/15/92	OTHER

TOTAL $100,311.74

SHIP TO

Flastinhagen Flintin Foundry
A Division of The Flimber Company
70809 Uniform Road
Irregular, NX 76999

APPROVED BY _____   DATE _____

Purchase Order

Disk File Name

OPR_12.XLS

Using This Form

This is a two-up purchase order form, designed to produce two short purchase orders with each printing. If you wish to print only a single purchase order, change the print area to exclude the second PO. (Use Options Set Print Area.)

Entering Data

Enter dates as values [1] or with the DATE function. Make sure you use a format that Excel recognizes as a date.

Printing This Form

Click the printer tool in the toolbar or choose Print from the File menu.

The FLIMBER Company
ADDRESS1
CITY STATE ZIP

ADDRESS2
PHONE

PURCHASE ORDER #   999999

SHIP TO

QTY.	PLEASE SUPPLY THE ITEMS BELOW	UNIT PRICE	AMOUNT
555	Screw Cap Sorters	$1.55	$860.25

FOB TIJUANA
SHIP VIA PONY XPRESS
DATE 12/12/92 ❶
TERMS 2 / 10 N 30

TO

Annie's Vermont Condiments
Ketchup Division
456 Old Country Way
Moonachie, NJ 00090

DATE REQUIRED   7/9/92
Please notify us immediately if you are unable
to ship the complete order by the date specified.
IMPORTANT
Purchase Order Number [999999]
must appear on all invoices,
acknowledgments, bills of
lading, correspondence, and
shipping cartons.
Please send 2 copies of your invoice

AUTHORIZED SIGNATURE

- -

Company Name
ADDRESS1
CITY STATE ZIP

ADDRESS2
PHONE

PURCHASE ORDER # JJ-2

SHIP TO

QTY.	PLEASE SUPPLY THE ITEMS BELOW	UNIT PRICE	AMOUNT

FOB
SHIP VIA
DATE
TERMS

TO

DATE REQUIRED   7/9/92
Please notify us immediately if you are unable
to ship the complete order by the date specified.
IMPORTANT
Purchase Order Number [JJ-2]
must appear on all invoices,
acknowledgments, bills of
lading, correspondence, and
shipping cartons.
Please send 2 copies of your invoice

AUTHORIZED SIGNATURE

Vendor Master File

Disk File Name

OPR_13.XLS

Using This Form

Use the Vendor Master File to record all purchases from a given vendor. Use the Remarks column to record important points that will
enable you to evaluate a vendor.

Entering Data

Enter data into this form either manually or in the worksheet. There
are no calculations in the form.

Printing This Form

Click the printer tool in the toolbar or choose Print from the File
menu.

VENDOR MASTER FILE

VENDOR NAME

KMT Software, Inc

CONTACT

Buck O'Day

ADDRESS

999 California St / SF CA 90909

PHONE

(415)-777-7777

CAPACITY Unlimited   CREDIT RATING AAA   OUR RATING AAA+++

DELIVERY TIME

FREIGHT 3 days   EXPRESS overnight   TRUCK 2 days

DATE	PURCHASE ORDER #	MATERIAL	PART NUMBER	QUANTITY	REMARKS
05/09/92	0909098	Diskette Sleeves	DS-9999	5,000	Might be short
07/09/92	878787	Monitor Collars	MC - 0987	33,566	Tight, but we won't choke

Backorder Control

Disk File Name

OPR_14.XLS

Using This Form

Use this form to track items that you have ordered but that have not yet been delivered. Whenever you plan to place an order, check this report first to make sure you have not already placed it.

Entering Data

Enter all data into unprotected cells. Be sure to enter the quantities on orders and backorders as values so that the Total column can be calculated. Dates [1] can be entered as values or with the DATE function.

Printing This Form

Click the printer tool in the toolbar or choose Print from the File menu.

BACKORDER CONTROL

	PERIOD	
	FROM	TO
	08/01/92	09/17/92

❶

ITEM NUMBER	DESCRIPTION	QUANTITY		TOTAL	DATE		
		ON ORDER	BACKORDERS		ORDERED	DUE	RECEIVED
0099	Gilded Lilies	5,000	1,000	6,000	8/1/92	9/3/92	
9876	Garlic Presses	1,200	155	1,355	8/13/92	9/17/92	

SIGNED _____

Shipping Order

Disk File Name

OPR_15.XLS

Using This Form

Use this form to tell the shipping department to assemble an order and prepare it for shipment to a customer. Customers should receive a copy of the form since it informs them of important information, such as their order numbers.

Entering Data

You may enter data into the worksheet, or print the form and enter the data by hand. Cells F34 to I35 [1] form an unprotected range where you can enter messages such as the interest statement included in the form.

Printing This Form

Click the printer tool in the toolbar or choose Print from the File menu.

The FLIMBER Company   SHIPPING ORDER

SOLD TO
Aunt Bea's Atomic Mustard Plasters
1010 Fifth Street
Reactor Building
Painesville OH 09090

CUSTOMER NO.
TERMS | 2 / 10 N 30
SALES
APPROX SHIP WEEK
DATE SHIPPED
FOB | St. Louis, MO
ROUTING

SHIP TO
Aunt Bea's Atomic Mustard Plasters
1010 Fifth Street
Reactor Building
Painesville OH 09090

Interest will be charged at the rate of 1.5% per month, ❶
equaling an annual rate of 18%.

ABD 09	4/14/93	UT 098
YOUR ORDER NUMBER	ORDER DATE	OUR ORDER NO.

ITEM	QUANTITY ORDERED	DESCRIPTION	QUANTITY SHIPPED	NO. OF CARTONS	TOTAL WEIGHT	PACKED BY (INITS)
U-235	12	Enriched Plutonium lbs	8	1	11	
PB 199	86	Refined Lead Linings	82	24	241	
AU 090	3	Pyrite Wimple Dishes	2	1	87.5	
TOTALS			92	26	339.5	

PACKED BY   DATE   CHECKED BY   DATE

INSTRUCTIONS:

1. PACK AND SHIP THE ABOVE PRODUCTS TO THE CUSTOMER'S SHIP TO ADDRESS PROVIDED ABOVE.
2. PLACE PACKING LIST IN SHIPPING CONTAINER.
3. RETURN ONE COPY OF THIS FORM TO OFFICE ON THE DAY OF SHIPMENT.

Bill of Lading

Disk File Name

OPR_16.XLS

Using This Form

This form should be used in duplicate (or triplicate), with one copy to accompany the shipment, and one to be retained by the shipper. A third copy may be required by the carrier as proof of delivery.

Entering Data

You may prepare this form in the worksheet or fill it out by hand. Enter data into unprotected cells.

Printing This Form

Click the printer tool in the toolbar or choose Print from the File menu.

The FLIMBER Company

The Finest in Flanges and Brackets
Fifty five Flimber Way
Lorain OH 99999

Bill of Lading

No.:   **15958**

FROM				TO	
Name	Clint Flint			Name	Noyes E. Croude
				Company	Yellin, Holleran, and Shoutz
				Street	9876 B Street
Date	7/6/93			City, State	Needles CA
Dept	Flash Trimming	Acct	3847	Zip Code	98989-0987

Number of Packages	Kind of Package, Description of Articles, Special Marks, and Exceptions	Weight (Subject to Change)	Serial Numbers	
1	Large Crated Sounding Box	987	NA	

Shipping Instructions				For Shipping Use Only	
Check One		Payment		Method	Date
	Next Day		Shipper	Bill No.	Shipped By
	Second Day		Recipient	Ship. Cost	Dept. Chgd
X	Routine		Third Party		
			COD Amt Due		

Delivered by		Date	
Received by		Date	# Boxes

COMMENTS

Deliver by Wednesday if possible, otherwise, try by next Monday or later.

Receiving Report

Disk File Name

OPR_17.XLS

Using This Form

Use this form to document what you received, when you received it, and the condition of goods shipped to you from vendors.

Entering Data

This form is primarily designed to be filled in manually. You may fill in heading data such as the name and address of the vendor, your PO number [1], and so forth, at the time a PO is cut, then file a copy of the partially completed form in a tickler file for transmission to the receiving department when the shipment is due.

Printing This Form

Click the printer tool in the toolbar or choose Print from the File menu.

RECEIVING REPORT

Fred's Fasteners and Fishing Supplies
RECEIVED FROM

04/03/93
DATE

Second
SHIFT

999 Haddock Hill Road
ADDRESS

Gloucester MA 09090
CITY/ST/ZIP

Same
SHIPPED FROM

CHECK CARRIER (note and detail OTHER)

☐ UNITED PARCEL SVC	☐ SHIPPER'S TRUCK
☐ PARCEL POST (USPS)	☐ AIR EXPRESS
☒ TRUCK	☐ EXPRESS MAIL
☐ RAIL	☐ OTHER

☐ PREPAID   ☒ COLLECT $999.00

OUR ORDER NUMBER	DATE SHIPPED	SHIPPED TO ATTENTION OF	LOCATION	PHONE
LDC 999999 ❶	04/15/92	Al Ternatev	Upstairs	x999

QTY	DESCRIPTION	NUMBER OF CARTONS	WEIGHT EACH	WEIGHT TOTAL	CARTON CONDITION	REC'D BY INTLS
65,000	Flimbered Snap Rings	65	87	5,655	Good	MCL
650	Haddock Cleaners	12	32	384	Wet/Torn	CSM

SHIPMENT COMPLETE or PARTIAL	TOTAL NUMBER OF CARTONS	TOTAL WEIGHT	NUMBER & CONDITION OF ITEMS REC'D OKAY	DAMAGED
Complete	77	6,039	345	(268)

RECEIVED BY	DATE	RECEIVED IN OFFICE BY	DATE
CHECKED BY	DATE	AUDITED BY	DATE

Inspection Report

Disk File Name

OPR_18.XLS

Using This Form

Use this form to document the condition of shipments you receive from your vendors. The form can then be used to document any possible damage for which you need to negotiate a claim or seek an insurance settlement.

Entering Data

This form is designed to be filled in manually.

Printing This Form

Click the printer tool in the toolbar or choose Print from the File menu.

INSPECTION REPORT

Phranque Phinque
RECEIVED FROM

55 Fessenden
ADDRESS

Philadelphia   PA   09090
CITY STATE and ZIP

Fredricksburg
SHIPPED FROM

January 12, 1993
DATE

First
SHIFT

CHECK CARRIER (note and detail OTHER)

☐	UNITED PARCEL SERVICE	☐	SHIPPER'S TRUCK
☐	PARCEL POST (USPS)	☐	AIR EXPRESS
x	TRUCK	☐	EXPRESS MAIL
☐	RAIL	☐	OTHER

INSPECTED

x	ON DOCK	☐	IN QUALITY CONTROL

QUANTITY RECEIVED	QUANTITY ACCEPTED	QUANTITY REJECTED
875	868	7

		INSPECTION ACTION			
ITEM	DESCRIPTION	APPROVED	REJECTED	REASON	DISPOSITION RECOMMENDED
1	Round Red Wrapping Spools	600	none	All good	Keep and use
2	Long Lumber Lacings	268	7	Seven splintered	Sand and save
3					
4					
5					
6					
7					
8					
9					
10					
11					
12					
13					
14					
15					
16					

INSPECTED BY	DATE	RECEIVED IN OFFICE BY	DATE	OUR PURCHASE ORDER NO.
Phil Frankel	1/15/93	Fanny Flimber	1/16/93	
CHECKED BY	DATE	AUDITED BY	DATE	DISPOSITION CODES
Fred Fenton	1/15/93	Ferd Fellows	1/16/93	RETURN TO SUPPLIER rs
APPROVED BY	DATE	ACCTNG DISPOSITION BY	DATE	REWORK & BILL SUPPLIER rb
Fawn Federing	1/16/93	Phineas Faust		SCRAP sc

Receipt For Goods

Disk File Name

OPR_19.XLS

Using This Form

Use this form to record goods shipped to you by vendors. Any problems with or damage to the shipment should be recorded on this form, so that adjustments or credits can be documented when the invoice arrives.

Entering Data

This form is designed to be completed by hand.

Printing This Form

Click the printer tool in the toolbar or choose Print from the File menu.

The FLIMBER Company
The Finest in Brackets and Flanges

RECEIPT FOR GOODS

Walken, Clymen, and Runze
RECEIVED FROM

22 Irving Street
ADDRESS

_____
ADDRESS

Newark   NJ   07998
CITY   STATE   ZIP

DATE 11/15/94

OUR P.O. # 999

CHARGES

PREPAID 11.85

COLLECT _____

FOR DEPT. Casting

JOB NO. 6009

REQ. NO. 87-009

DELIVERED BY (CARRIER NAME)	BILL OF LADING NUMBER	FREIGHT BILL NUMBER
Stille Trucking	098-098	FBN000009

X Freight	Air Freight	Express	Air Express	Local Delivery	
P.P.	Air P.P.	Pick-Up	Messenger		

FOR OFFICE USE ONLY

INVOICE NUMBER

INVOICE DATE

CASES	CARTONS	PACKAGES	CRATES	BUNDLES	DRUMS	BAGS	OTHER
			99				

TOTAL # PACKAGES	TOTAL WEIGHT	PARTIAL	COMPLETE

	QUANTITY	DESCRIPTION	CONDITION	WEIGHT	ENTERED
1	88	Blister pack bubble pads	Good	2.5 lbs	
2	10	Ground wire assemblies	"	81 lbs	
3	1	Sample set of freezer flanges	"	13 oz	
4					
5					
6					
7					
8					
9					
10					
11					
12					
13					
14					
15					

REMARKS

_____   _____
RECEIVED BY   **CHECKED BY**

Invoice Record

Disk File Name

OPR_20.XLS

Using This Form

This form tracks all invoices you receive from a given customer, as well as the key actions you take on them. In effect, the form is a database of your transactions with that vendor. It also lets you keep track of why you deducted payments from an invoice.

Entering Data

Enter data into unprotected cells. Enter dates [1] either as values or labels.

Printing This Form

Click the printer tool in the toolbar or choose Print from the File menu.

INVOICE RECORD

COMPANY The Flimber Company

ADDRESS 663 Old Fedora Highway, Flimber MN 09090

A/R CONTACT Sue Blime

A/R PHONE 777-999-0000

FAX 777-999-9999

Order Number	Invoice Number	Date ❶	Date Received	Amount	Deductions	Net Passed	Discount Date	Date Passed	By	Remarks
TR-0990	UB-0090	09/03/93	08/08/92	$1,234.56	$152.22	$1,082.34	8/26/93	08/31/93	HST	Short shipment
BR-01010	UM-2311	09/19/93	08/26/93	2,345.67	15.25	2,330.42	9/14/93	09/16/93	JEK	Shipping Damage
IMSR -090	UC-0099	10/07/93	09/14/93	3,210.98	367.47	2,843.51	10/02/93	10/03/93	JCM	Crated improperly

PC Tracking Sheet

Disk File Name

OPR_21.XLS

Using This Form

This form allows you to record the characteristics of all the personal computers in your company or department, to improve the effectiveness of technical support. The forms can be filled out by hand or electronically.

Entering Data

Enter data into unprotected cells. Enter the date in cell K23 [1]. Be sure you use a date format that Excel recognizes.

Printing This Form

Click the printer tool in the toolbar or choose Print from the File menu.

PC Tracking Sheet

❶

Physical Location
Date: 13 Nov 93

Assigned to	Title	Dept	Location
"Sly" Drule	Staff Researcher	R&D	MDF

System Unit

Manufacturer	Model	Serial Number	OS & Version
RaceWay 500	586 PF Flyer	RW-7362-H : 6JK-124	DOS 6.01
Processor & Speed	Math Chip	ROM BIOS & Version	RAM & Configuration
80586 / 100 MHz	Whytek 1492	PHELIX 7.4	64 MB w/1MB Cache

Input Devices

Keyboard	Mouse	Track Ball	Other:
RaceWay 136	"Mickey" (1600 DPI)		

Monitor

Manufacturer	Model	Serial Number	Type
RaceWay	PFX	PJS-748932-KJ8	XGA Plus

Drives

Drive A Size & Capacity	Drive B Size & Capacity	Other Floppy Drive Size & Capacity
3.5" 1.44MB	5.25" 1.2MB	
Hard Drive C Capacity	Hard Drive D Capacity	Other Hard Drive Capacity
600 MB		

Backup / Removable Media Manufacturer & Model	Serial Number	Capacity
Burn-Newly Jet Portable	YT123-QW845635767864	180MB

Adapters and Controllers

Display Adapter	Memory Expansion Card	Hard Disk Controller	Backup Controller
XGA Plus			
Accelerator / Turbo	Network	Fax / Modem	Scanner
	4LPT		ICU Scanner Pro

Peripherals

Tape Drive	Printer	Label / Envelope Printer	Other:
Modem	Scanner	Surge Suppresser	Other:
		Hydrophenia	

Software

Shell / Multitasker	Word Processor	Spreadsheet	Other:
"Winduhs" 4.1	BytePerfect	XL (what else?)	
Database	Graphics	Utilities	Other:
CumuloNimbus	Yale	Mansfield	
Device Drivers (attach CONFIG.SYS)		Memory Resident Programs (attach AUTOEXEC.BAT)	
Lots of them. See printout.		Lots of them. See printout.	

CHAPTER
6

PERSONAL FORMS

In this section you will find a variety forms and files designed to help you manage your personal affairs. Though most of the forms address important financial topics, such as mortgage costs, mortgages refinancing , and calculating the cost of a college education, a few deal with more prosaic topics such as keeping track of what's on your videotapes, and how you are progressing in an exercise plan.

Personal Budget

Disk File Name

PER_01.XLS

Using This Form

This form is used for your personal financial planning. It includes many categories of income and expenses, and can be customized to suit your particular needs. Due to the numerous calculations, the form is intended to be used electronically. However, you could print it and rough out the numbers on paper before entering them into the computer.

Entering Data

Enter annual figures [1] into unprotected cells in the form. Monthly figures [2] and percentages [3] are calculated automatically. Because the line item descriptions [4] are unprotected, you can change any description simply by typing over it.

Printing This Form

Click the printer tool in the toolbar or choose Print from the File menu.

Adapting This Form

Though the Personal Budget form will handle most categories of income and expense, you may wish to add or subtract line items. To do so, choose Options Unprotect Document (or type Alt OP), and simply insert or delete rows.

It's best to avoid inserting at the top of ranges, as the total formulas will not automatically adjust to include the new data. After you have inserted a new row, copy the formats and formulas from the already existing rows.

Design Notes

Blank rows have been used above and below the separator lines to provide white space and make the totals more visible.

Personal Budget
For 1993

INCUME	❶ ANNUAL	❷ MONTHLY	❸ %
Salary #1	$64,000	$5,333	46%
Bonus #1	5,000	417	4%
Salary #2	48,000	4,000	35%
Bonus #2	2,000	167	1%
❹ Estimated Stock Options	12,000	1,000	9%
Dividends	2,000	167	1%
Interest	500	42	0%
Tax Refund	700	58	1%
Other: Summer Rental	4,500	375	3%
Other:	0	0	0%
TOTAL INCOME	**$138,700**	**$11,559**	**100%**

EXPENSES	ANNUAL	MONTHLY	%
Charitable Donations	$5,400	$450	4%
Taxes & Withholding	26,400	2,200	19%
Groceries	14,000	1,167	10%
Mortgage	21,600	1,800	16%
Property Tax	2,000	167	1%
Utilities	4,000	333	3%
Home Maintenance	2,000	167	1%
Clothing & Dry Cleaning	4,000	333	3%
Uninsured Medical & Dental	700	58	1%
Child Care	5,000	417	4%
Car Loans	7,600	633	5%
Gasoline & Oil	1,250	104	1%
Car Repairs & Maintenance	600	50	0%
Other Loans & Credit Cards	6,400	533	5%
Major Purchases	4,500	375	3%
Telephone	1,080	90	1%
Insurance: Life, Fire, Car	1,700	142	1%
Savings	5,000	417	4%
Investments	8,000	667	6%
Vacation	4,000	333	3%
Books, CDs, Magazines	650	54	0%
Fitness & Entertainment	1,200	100	1%
Personal Grooming	1,200	100	1%
Tuition	3,500	292	3%
Gifts	4,200	350	3%
Miscellaneous	2,000	167	1%
TOTAL EXPENSES	**$137,980**	**$11,499**	**99%**
SURPLUS OR SHORTFALL	**$720**	**$60**	**1%**

Statement of Net Worth

Disk File Name

PER_02.XLS

Using This Form

This form is a "snapshot" of your financial condition. The version shown here may be more detailed than you need, but it is easy to adapt.

Entering Data

Enter all data into the unprotected cells in column E [1]. Note that all line-item descriptions [2] are also unprotected, making them easy to change.

Printing This Form

Click the printer tool in the toolbar or choose Print from the File menu.

Adapting This Form

The line items in the Statement of Net Worth form are unprotected, allowing you to make most changes without modifications. However, if you have many more or fewer entries, you may wish to add or subtract line items. To do so, choose Options Unprotect Document (or type Alt OP), and simply insert or delete rows.

It's best to avoid inserting at the top of ranges, as the total formulas will not automatically adjust to include the new data. After you have inserted a new row, copy the formats and formulas from the already existing rows. Be sure to reset the row height for consistency with the other rows.

Design Notes

The dark shaded separating lines [3] were created by reducing the heights of certain rows and setting the color of some cells to dark blue.

Statement of Net Worth

Juan R. Full
12/31/92

❶

ASSETS

		CURRENT VALUE	% OF TOTAL ASSETS
Liquid Assets	Cash (checking, savings accounts)	$1,900	0.20%
	Short-Term Investments	5,400	0.56%
	Treasury Bills	2,000	0.21%
	Savings Certificates ❷	18,000	1.86%
	Money Market Funds	2,500	0.26%
	Cash Value of Life Insurance	16,500	1.71%
	Total Liquid Assets	$46,300	4.79%
❸	Notes receivable		
Investment Assets	Marketable Securities	32,500	3.36%
	Stocks	6,000	0.62%
	Bonds	8,000	0.83%
	Real Estate (investment)	16,000	1.65%
	Tax Incentive Investments	6,000	0.62%
	Value of Stock in DF Enterprises, Inc.	158,500	16.38%
	Retirement Funds	85,000	8.79%
	Total Investment Assets	$312,000	32.25%
Personal Assets	Residence	$385,991	39.90%
	Vacation Property	158,000	16.33%
	Art, Antiques	26,000	2.69%
	Furnishings	12,500	1.29%
	Vehicles	25,855	2.67%
	Boats	650	0.07%
	Other	100	0.01%
	Total Personal Assets	$609,096	62.96%
	TOTAL ASSETS	**$967,396**	**100.00%**

LIABILITIES

		CURRENT VALUE	% OF TOTAL LIABILITIES
Short Term	Consumer Credit Obligations	$1,234	0.77%
	Borrowings on Life Insurance	1,200	0.75%
	Installment Loans	6,500	4.05%
	Personal Guarantee		
	Accrued Income Taxes	4,500	2.81%
	Other Debt	1,500	0.94%
	Total Short-Term Liabilities	$14,934	9.31%
Long Term	Loans to Purchase Personal Assets	$61,000	38.04%
	Loan to Acquire Business	444	0.28%
	Mortgage on Personal Residences	84,000	52.38%
	Total Long-Term Liabilities	145,444	90.69%
	TOTAL LIABILITIES	**$160,378**	**100.00%**
	TOTAL NET WORTH	**$807,018**	

Investment Goals and Performance

Disk File Name

PER_03.XLS

Using This Form

This form serves as both a review and an inventory of your current investments. Use it either on paper or electronically.

Entering Data

Enter the date [1], the type of asset [2], your cost [3], the current value [4], the objective [5] met by the investment, and the income it provides [6]. All other figures are calculated.

Printing This Form

Click the printer tool in the toolbar or choose Print from the File menu.

Adapting This Form

If you have more than fifteen investments, you may wish to add more line items to this form. However, before you expend the time and energy to do so, consider using several copies of the form—one for each type of investment you own. Remember to give each file a different name.

If you do decide to add more rows, you'll be able to make the most of the available space by resetting row heights. You will then be able to insert about ten more rows without adjusting the print margins or resorting to print scaling.

Then, unprotect the worksheet and simply insert rows. It's best to avoid inserting rows at the top of ranges, as the total formulas will not automatically adjust to include the new data. After you have inserted the new rows, copy the formats and formulas from the already existing rows.

Investment Goals and Performance

❶ Bill and Sally Forth
9/1/92

IMPORTANCE Indicate the relative importance you place on the following considerations by entering the appropriate number after each question.

Unimportant 1
Somewhat important 2
Important 3
Very important 4
Extremely important 5

DIVERSITY How important is it to avoid big losses by spreading your risk? `1`

LIQUIDITY How important is it to have ready cash for emergencies or opportunities? `4`

SAFETY If the country entered a deep depression, how important would it be to sell your investments at roughly the price you paid? `5`

INCOME Is it important to maximize your investment income this year and next? `4`

APPRECIATION Is it important that your investments keep pace with or do better than inflation? `3`

TAX ADVANTAGE Is it important to get maximum tax relief available? `2`

LEVERAGE How important do you think it is to borrow money in the hope of reaping a higher return on investment? `1`

\NAGEMENT EASE How important is it not to have to watch or worry about your investments? `2`

❷ TYPE OF ASSET	❸ VALUE ACQUIRED	CURRENT	% OF TOTAL	❺ OBJECTIVE	CURR. INCOME	APPR'N (LOSS)	❻ INCOME AS % TOTAL	CURRENT
KMT Common Stock	$2,500	$31,500	14.3%	Growth	$2,850	$29,000	114.00%	9.05%
Oat Bran Bonds	5,200	125	0.1%	Diversity	2	(5,075)	0.03%	1.28%
Hh Real Estate	189,500	187,500	85.2%	Income	13,500	(2,000)	7.12%	7.20%
Coins	218	1,021	0.5%	Appreciation	0	803	0.00%	0.00%
TOTAL	$197,418	$220,146	100%		$16,352	$22,728	8.28%	10.32%

Capital Gains and Losses

Disk File Name

PER_04.XLS

Using This Form

This form will help you to keep track of the disposition of your investments. At year end, use it to see if you have any investment losses that may be used to offset gains.

Entering Data

Enter data into the appropriate columns. In Net Proceeds [1], enter the amount you realize from a sale, not the price for which you sell.

Printing This Form

Click the printer tool in the toolbar or choose Print from the File menu.

Adapting This Form

If you have more than ten transactions or securities in your current portfolio, you may consider adding more line items to this form.

Perhaps the best way to do that is to turn the form into a two-page report. First, unprotect the worksheet. Then, insert twenty rows in the top section of the form. It's best to avoid inserting rows at the top of ranges [2], as the total formulas will not automatically adjust to include the new data. After you have inserted the new rows, copy the formats and formulas from the already existing rows. Next, choose Format Row Height to set the row height to 16, for consistency with the other rows. Finally, just below the Net Capital Gain or Loss figure [3], use the Options Set Page Break command to force a page break.

Add 25 rows to the Unrealized Gains or Losses section using the same techniques as above, remembering to copy the formats and set the row heights.

Capital Gains and Losses

MICAH FREEMAN

4/9/93

GAINS AND LOSSES REALIZED TO DATE

NUMBER OF UNITS	INVESTMENT TYPE	PRICE PER UNIT	DATE ACQUIRED	AMOUNT INVESTED	DATE SOLD	NET PROCEEDS ❶	GAIN OR (LOSS) ❸
1	Berkshire Hathaway	2,400	11/15/87	2,400	12/30/91	$8,152	$5,752 ❷
10	IBM Bonds	1,200	06/03/90	12,000	12/30/91	15,055	3,055
300	Prune Futures Fund	11	10/14/89	3,200	12/30/91	1,400	(1,800)
200	Reading Railroad	31	07/11/84	6,200	12/30/91	5,000	(1,200)
2,000	Water Company	23	08/16/88	46,000	12/30/91	35,250	(10,750)
2	Atlantic City Bonds	6,000	08/04/89	12,000	12/30/91	14,000	2,000

NET GAIN OR (LOSS)	($2,943)
CAPITAL LOSS CARRYOVERS	$4,000
NET CAPITAL GAIN OR (LOSS)	($6,943)

UNREALIZED GAINS OR LOSSES IN CURRENT INVESTMENTS

NUMBER OF UNITS	INVESTMENT TYPE	DATE ACQUIRED	COST PER UNIT	TOTAL COST OR BASIS	CURRENT MARKET PRICE	CURRENT MARKET VALUE	GAIN OR (LOSS)
200	Apple Computer	02/28/90	45.00	$9,000	55.00	$11,000	$2,000 ❷
1,500	Novell	08/17/90	26.75	40,125	52.88	79,313	39,188
1,000	Symbolics	06/25/91	1.25	1,250	1.08	1,075	(175)

NET UNREALIZED CAPITAL GAIN OR (LOSS)	$41,013

Income-Planning Worksheet

Disk File Name

PER_05.XLS

Using This Form

Use this form at or near the beginning of the year to lay out an overall strategy. Once you have outlined your income goals, translate them into an action plan that you can record on the Yearly Planner Form.

Entering Data

Use your Federal Income Tax Form 1040 as the source of most of the values in column C [1].

Printing This Form

Click the printer tool in the toolbar or choose Print from the File menu.

Adapting This Form

You can make this form more powerful and customize it to your needs by linking some of the data input cells to more detailed calculations, either elsewhere in the worksheet, or in other worksheet files.

Here's how to link an input cell to another file. If, for example, you wish to build up the Capital Gain or Loss [2] entry (cell E27) from a more detailed analysis, you can enter a formula that references the previous file, PER_04. It would look something like this: =PER_04!H44. Naturally, the filename and cell address will vary if you have renamed the Capital Gains file and/or changed its layout.

If you want to create a series of calculations directly in the Income Planning Worksheet, simply go to an area of the file that is not in use, unprotect the worksheet, and enter your formulas and data (for example, to determine Capital Gain or Loss). Enter a cell reference (for example, in cell E27) to bring the desired amount into the Income Planning calculations.

Income Planning Worksheet

A. Tom McEnnergie **❶**

Gross Income	LAST YEAR	THIS YEAR
Taxable Wages/Salaries	$65,800	$82,500
Taxable Dividends and Interest	1,300	1,384
Net Business Income (Loss)		
❷ Net Capital Gain (Loss)	1,700	(5,200)
Net Rent Income (Loss)	(14,455)	(13,855)
Net Partnership Income (Loss)	3,000	3,100
Other Income (Loss)	225	(150)
TOTAL Gross Income	57,570	67,779
Adjustments to Gross Income		
Alimony Paid		
IRA Payments	2,000	3,200
Keogh Plan Payments	3,000	3,100
Deduction for Married Couple When Both Work		
Other Adjustments		
TOTAL Adjustments to Gross Income	5,000	6,300
Adjusted Gross Income	$52,570	$61,479
Allowable Itemized Deductions		
Medical	186	30
Taxes	4,786	5,400
Mortgage Interest Paid	7,412	7,300
Other Interest Paid	1,600	400
Charitable Contributions	257	400
Casualty and Theft Losses		
Unreimbursed Moving Expenses		4,800
Unreimbursed Employee Business Deductions		1,000
Miscellaneous Deductions	241	150
TOTAL Itemized Deductions	14,482	19,480
Standard Deduction		
Greater of Itemized Deductions or Std Deduction	14,482	
Allowable Exemptions (number)	4	4
Allowable Exemptions ($ value)	2,150	2,200
TOTAL Deductions and Exemptions	23,082	
Taxable Income	29,488	
Tax Bracket		
Targeted Taxable Income		
Targeted Tax Bracket		

Notes: Date: 05/12/93

Discretionary Income Plan

Disk File Name

PER_06.XLS

Using This Form

Use this form to set a personal disposable income goal; it will help you to get a handle on expenses.

Entering Data

Enter all data directly into the worksheet. Percentages are calculated automatically.

Printing This Form

Click the printer tool in the toolbar or choose Print from the File menu.

Adapting This Form

The Discretionary Income form will handle the most common types of expenditures, though you may wish to customize the form to your particular circumstances. Most changes can be made by simply unprotecting the form and typing over the protected line-item descriptions.

If you decide to insert additional rows, remember to set the heights of the new rows, for consistency. It's best to avoid inserting at the top of ranges, as the total formulas will not automatically adjust to include the new data. After you have inserted the new row, use the Copy command to copy the formats and formulas from the already existing rows.

Discretionary Income Plan

Dr. Mike Roskopik, TNY
1992

	AMOUNT	PERCENT
EDUCATION (Private Secondary Schools and College)		
Michael	16,000	16.58%
Sandy	8,000	8.29%
Lauren	8,000	8.29%
Kevin	2,500	2.59%
ENTERTAINMENT AND EATING OUT	1,800	1.87%
REGULAR VACATIONS	4,500	4.66%
EXTRAORDINARY CHARITABLE EXPENDITURES	500	0.52%
HOBBIES	3,000	3.11%
PERSONAL GIFTS	1,250	1.30%
SUPPORT OF RELATIVES AND OTHERS		
Mrs. Thelma Louise	6,000	6.22%
Mr. Holden Caulfield	1,200	1.24%
HOME IMPROVEMENTS	3,500	3.63%
PURCHASE OF AUTOMOBILES, BOATS, ETC.	4,850	5.03%
RETIREMENT PLANS		
IRA	2,000	2.07%
KEOGH	16,000	16.58%
OTHER	12,000	12.44%
DEBT REDUCTION	2,400	2.49%
OTHER	3,000	3.11%
TOTAL Discretionary Expenditures	96,500	
AVERAGE Monthly Amount	8,042	

Year-End Tax Plan

Disk File Name

PER_07.XLS

Using This Form

This form can serve two purposes: as a year-end tax planner, and to prepare quarterly tax payments, if necessary. As a year-end tool, it helps you to determine where you will be financially at the end of the year so that you can take advantage of capital losses (see the Capital Gains and Losses form). And, with an approximation of your adjusted gross income, you can more efficiently calculate a quarterly payment.

Entering Data

Using the most recent tax data available, enter the amount of the standard deduction in cell C19. All of the remaining data [1] should be entered directly onto the form.

Printing This Form

Click the printer tool in the toolbar or choose Print from the File menu.

Year-End Tax Plan

M. T. Ouellette
August 1992

		ESTIMATES	
	To Date	To Year End	Full Year
GROSS INCOME			
Taxable Wages/Salaries	$36,000 ❶	$41,000	$77,000
Taxable Dividends and Interest		1,850	1,850
Net Business Income (Loss)	1,500	17,500	19,000
Net Capital Gain (Loss)		(500)	(500)
Net Rent Income (Loss)	(785)	(8,975)	(9,760)
Net Partnership Income (Allowable Loss)	200	11,000	11,200
Other Income (Loss)		500	500
TOTAL Gross Income	36,915	62,375	99,290
ADJUSTMENTS TO GROSS INCOME			
Alimony Paid			
IRA Payments	200	1,800	2,000
Keogh Plan Payments	500	2,600	3,100
Other Adjustments		100	100
TOTAL Adjustments	700	4,500	5,200
ADJUSTED GROSS INCOME	$36,215	$57,875	$94,090
ALLOWABLE ITEMIZED DEDUCTIONS			
Medical		$1,500	$1,500
Taxes	1,500	6,800	8,300
Mortgage Interest Paid	1,575	6,825	8,400
Charitable Contributions		1,200	1,200
Casualty and Theft Losses			
Unreimbursed Moving Expenses			
Unreimbursed Employee Business Expen:	85	600	685
Miscellaneous Deductions			
TOTAL Itemized Deductions	$3,160	$16,925	$20,085
Greater of Itemized Deductions or Std Deduction			20,085
Value of Exemptions	$2,150		
Number of Allowable Exemptions	4		8,600
TOTAL Deductions and Exemptions			$28,685

Taxable Income	$65,405
Tax Bracket	35.00%
Targeted Taxable Income	$57,000
Targeted Tax Bracket	25.00%

Mortgage Amortization

Disk File Name

PER_08.XLS

Using This Form

Use this form to calculate the monthly payments and first-year amortization schedule for a mortgage. The form also calculates the first year's tax deduction from the amortization schedule. Due to the large number of formulas, this form is intended to be used only electronically.

Entering Data

Enter data into the unprotected cells [1]. There is space for the principal, the interest rate (enter percentages as decimals), the number of months of the loan, and the base month and year of the loan. All the rest of the form is calculated automatically.

Printing This Form

Click the printer tool in the toolbar or choose Print from the File menu.

Formula Notes

The months of the calendar are determined by a lookup table located below and to the right of the amortization table. You need enter only the first three letters of a month [2] for the form to determine the starting month. Similarly, the first-year deductions are calculated by looking up the word December in the amortization table and referencing the cumulative interest paid.

Design Notes

The most striking features of this form are its bilateral symmetry and its use of white space. It is also useful to note that the lines [3] that frame the amortization table are created by very narrow (1 point) rows formatted with solid shading. The resulting lines are wider than the normal lines, but finer than the wide lines.

Mortgage Amortization

ASSUMPTIONS

Loan Principal Amount	$95,000.00
Annual Interest Rate	8.25%
Loan Period in Months	180
Base Year of Loan	1993
Base Month of Loan	July
Annual Loan Payments	$11,059.56
Monthly Payments	$921.63
First Year Deductions	$3,890.81

❶

FIRST YEAR OF PAYMENTS

❷   **❸**

Year	Month	Beginning Balance	Payments	Principal	Interest	Cumulative Principal	Cumulative Interest
1993	July	$95,000.00	$921.63	$268.50	$653.13	$268.50	**$653.13**
	August	94,731.50	921.63	270.35	651.28	538.85	**1,304.41**
	September	94,461.15	921.63	272.21	649.42	811.06	**1,953.83**
	October	94,188.94	921.63	274.08	647.55	1,085.14	**2,601.38**
	November	93,914.86	921.63	275.97	645.66	1,361.11	**3,247.04**
	December	93,638.89	921.63	277.86	643.77	1,638.97	**3,890.81**
1994	January	93,361.03	921.63	279.77	641.86	1,918.74	**4,532.67**
	February	93,081.26	921.63	281.70	639.93	2,200.44	**5,172.60**
	March	92,799.56	921.63	283.63	638.00	2,484.07	**5,810.60**
	April	92,515.93	921.63	285.58	636.05	2,769.65	**6,446.65**
	May	92,230.35	921.63	287.55	634.08	3,057.20	**7,080.73**
	June	91,942.80	921.63	289.52	632.11	3,346.72	**7,712.84**

Mortgage Refinancing

Disk File Name

PER_09.XLS

Using This Form

Use this form to analyze the opportunity to refinance a mortgage. The form assumes that the new mortgage will be equal to the balance on the old mortgage. If it is not, use the amount of the new mortgage. It also assumes that you are comparing fixed-rate mortgages. Do not use this form with an adjustable-rate mortgage, since it cannot give you a valid comparison.

Entering Data

Enter all data into the unprotected cells of the form. All of the entries in the Personal Facts [1] and Mortgage Facts [2] sections are data. Except for the cost of points, which is calculated from the entry in the Mortgage Facts section, all of the entries in the Refinancing Facts [3] section are also entered as data. The form returns the number of months [4] it takes for the difference in payments to equal the refinancing costs. Note that the potential savings assumes that points are deductible [5]. Whether you can or cannot deduct points depends on how they are defined in the mortgage agreement. As always, consult a professional advisor before undertaking a major commitment like a mortgage refinancing.

Printing This Form

Click the printer tool in the toolbar or choose Print from the File menu.

MORTGAGE REFINANCING

❶ PERSONAL FACTS

Marginal Tax Rate	31.00%
Resale Plan (Months)	48

❷ MORTGAGE FACTS

Original Mortgage	$75,000
Original Term (yrs.)	30
Current Mortgage Rate	10.38%
Months Paid	65
New Mortgage Rate	8.50%
New Term (yrs.)	30
Points	2.0

❸ REFINANCING FACTS

Application	$55
Title	150
Legal	550
Other	750
Points	1,447
Total Fees	$2,952

ANALYSIS

	Current	Proposed
Mortgage Amount	$72,347	$72,347
Mortgage Payment	679.33	556.28
❹ Months to Recover Refinancing Costs		24
Mortgage Balance at Resale	$69,178	$69,852
Principal Repaid to Resale	3,169	2,495
Total Payments to Resale	32,608	26,702
Total Interest to Resale	29,439	24,206
❺ Tax Deduction on Interest	9,126	7,504
Tax Deduction for Points		449
Net Interest Cost to Resale	20,313	16,254
Net Interest Savings (Cost)		$4,059
Interest Savings (Costs)		$1,107

College Costs

Disk File Name

PER_10.XLS

Using This Form

Use this form to begin a college funding plan for one or more children. If you have more than four children, you will have to run the form twice.

Entering Data

Make sure to enter percentages [1] as decimals (.06 for 6%). Some data applies to all children [2] (such as the inflation rate and the return on savings), while some can be applied to each child individually. The number of years in college [3] and current tuition costs [4], for example, can be applied generally or individually. Current savings, however, must be assigned individually.

Printing This Form

Click the printer tool in the toolbar or choose Print from the File menu.

COLLEGE COSTS

Date: **November 16, 1992**

	Andy	Mandy	Ellie	Kelly
Children's Names	Andy	Mandy	Ellie	Kelly
Year of Birth	1989	1985	1991	1990
Ages of Children this Year	3	7	1	2
Begin College Age	18	17	17	17
Number of Years until College	15	10	16	15
❸ Estimated Number of Years in College	5	4	4	4
Number of Years for Inflation Adjustment	15	10	16	15
❷ Estimated Annual Inflation Rate Between Now and End of Education	4.00%			
Inflation Factor	1.80	1.48	1.87	1.80
❹ Estimated Annual College Costs Today	$15,000		$12,000	
Estimated Annual Cost of College, Adjusted for Inflation	27,014	22,204	22,476	27,014
Adjusted Estimate of TOTAL Costs	135,071	88,815	89,903	108,057
Estimated After-Tax Rate of Return on Savings and Investments for Education ❶	8.00%			
Compounding Factor	3.17	2.16	3.43	3.17
Present Value of Current Education Savings	1,000	2,000	3,000	4,000
Future Value of Current Education Savings	3,172	4,318	10,278	12,689
Annual Amount to Invest for Education	$4,858	$5,833	$2,626	$3,512

Life Insurance Requirements

Disk File Name

PER_11.XLS

Using This Form

This form incorporates a technique called "capital needs analysis" to help you determine how much life insurance you may need. Always check with a professional advisor before making an important financial decision.

Entering Data

Enter data into column G [1]. The capital needs analysis requires you to estimate how much you can earn on capital, so enter that value as a decimal (.1 for 10 percent) in cell F19 (not shown in the illustration). The lower you make F19, the more insurance this form will show.

Printing This Form

Click the printer tool in the toolbar or choose Print from the File menu.

Design Notes

Though it's impossible to tell on the printed page, this form employs red text to denote negative values [2].

LIFE INSURANCE REQUIREMENTS

Cash Required Immediately ❶
Funeral	$8,500
Current bills	6,500
Administrative costs	3,000
Emergency fund for family expenses	25,000
Estate taxes	2,500
TOTAL	$45,500

Cash Available Immediately
Insurance proceeds	$25,000
Death benefits of retirement programs	2,000
Liquid assets	1,800
Other: Baseball card collection	1,500
Other	
TOTAL	$30,300

Net Cash Available (or Required) ($15,200) ❷

Assets Required for Mortgage and Children's Education
Mortgage outstanding	$72,500
Education	115,000
TOTAL	$187,500

Assets Available for Mortgage and Children's Education
Investment assets	$36,000
Personal assets convertible to cash	15,000
Other	5,000
TOTAL	$56,000

Net Resources Available (or Required) ($131,500)

Annual Living Expenses $36,000

Annual Income Available for Living Expenses
Income from assets	$1,200
Employment income of spouse	14,000
Other	7,200
TOTAL	$22,400

Annual Income Excess (or Deficiency) ($13,600)
Capital Required for Income Goal (@ 6.00%)

Additional Insurance Required
Immediate expense requirement	$15,200
Mortgage and education requirement	131,500
Capital required for income goal	
TOTAL	**$146,700**

Gross Estate

Disk File Name

PER_12.XLS

Using This Form

Use this form to list the assets in yours and your spouse's estates. The form assumes that jointly held property is evenly held by each spouse.

Entering Data

Enter estimates of the value of items into column C first [1]. Then enter the amounts owned jointly and by you into columns D [2] and E [3], respectively. The amount remaining is owned by your spouse and may be calculated or entered into column F [4]. When the form displays *NA* or Estimate? it means that columns D and E do not balance with column C. That may happen when you first enter or change data in the Estimate column.

Printing This Form

Click the printer tool in the toolbar or choose Print from the File menu.

Abe & Anna Splitt

9/30/92

Property Ownership And Gross Estate

	❶	❷	❸	❹
	Estimated		Ownership	
	Value	Joint	Self	Spouse
NET WORTH				
Liquid Assets (excluding Cash Value of Life Ins.)	100,000	75,000		25,000
Investment Assets (excluding Retirement Funds	100,000	78,000	22,000	
Personal Assets	100,000	100,000		
Total Assets	300,000	253,000	22,000	25,000
Liabilities				
	$300,000	$253,000	$22,000	$25,000
INSURANCE OWNED				
On Your Life	125,000			125,000
On Your Spouse's Life	10,000		10,000	
	$135,000		$10,000	$125,000
OTHER ESTATE ASSETS				
Retirement Plans	65,000	35,000	15,000	15,000
Other				
	$65,000	$35,000	$15,000	$15,000
TOTAL GROSS ESTATE	$500,000	$288,000	$47,000	$165,000
TOTAL GROSS ESTATE FOR YOU AND YOUR SPOUSE				
Your Gross Estate	191,000		191,000	
Your Spouse's Gross Estate	309,000			309,000
TOTAL	**$500,000**			

Household Inventory

Disk File Name

PER_13.XLS

Using This Form

Inventory your household possessions on this form for insurance purposes. File the completed form in your safe deposit box or at your office. Update it annually or more frequently to reduce the risk of loss from underreporting. This form can also be used on paper, so feel free to print copies for friends and relatives.

Entering Data

Enter the date [1] as a label, for example, "As of 15 September, 92" into cell A22, just below the title. Then enter data into the unprotected cells in the body of the form.

Printing This Form

Click the printer tool in the toolbar or choose Print from the File menu.

Adapting This Form

If your home contains many rooms, or if you just want to track more items than the form allows, it can be extended quite easily.

Unprotect the worksheet and insert as many additional rows as you need. Copy one of the rows already in the form to make the new rows, so that the new rows pick up the same formatting.

Try this technique to print multiple pages with a professional touch. Adjust the print area so that it includes all of the new rows, but excludes the top rows of the form [2], rows 21 through 25. Then, choose Options Set Print Titles and select these rows as the top border of the form. This will make them print on every page, making it easy to identify the contents of each column.

You can also add columns for purchase dates or estimated replacement cost.

Household Inventory

as of 15 November 1992

Room	Item	Manufacturer and Model	Serial Number	Cost	Value
Living	Couch	Savannah Concepts		950	600
	2 Chairs	Humboldt Designs		1,200	800
	Stereo Receiver	Spott	JC483920-W43	260	200
	Speakers	Boss 590	678-1WE8	430	350
	CD Player	Leeding Edge	Q562-9085	210	180
	Lamps	2 Floor, 3 Table lamps		300	250
	Wallhangings	Roberto Cuzco litho, 3 misc		800	1,250
	Coffee Table	Humboldt Designs		180	145
Dining					
Kitchen					
Bedrooms					
Laundry					
Office					
Garage					
			Totals	4,330	3,775

Credit Card Log

Disk File Name

> PER_14.XLS

Using This Form

> Use this form to track all of your credit, membership, and telephone cards. The form can be filled out on paper or electronically. However, since very little will likely change from year to year, it will save time to maintain the form in the spreadsheet.

Entering Data

> Enter data into unprotected cells. Column F uses the mmm-yy format, enabling the month and year to be displayed. You may enter dates as values or as formulas.

Printing This Form

> Click the printer tool in the toolbar or choose Print from the File menu.

Adapting This Form

> In addition to tracking credit cards, this form can be used to track all sorts of information, from parking ID cards to supermarket courtesy cards. Use one form for you and your spouse, or simply leave a blank space between each set of cards.

CREDIT CARD LOG

Name: Rich & Faye Muss

Date: February 28, 1993

Card	Card Number	Account #	Limit	Expires	Cust Service	Call if Lost	Comment
AMIX	3708 61931 51002		#N/A	May-93	800-555-1212	800-555-1212	
VASI	3750 024 845 06	3750 024 845 06	5,000	Jan-94	800-555-1212	800-555-1212	change banks for lower APR?
Xonn	502 914 743 0 4 001		1,200	Feb-95	800-555-1212	800-555-1212	
Ceeres	04 22905 25489 6	04 22905 25489 6	3,000	NA	800-555-1212	800-555-1212	

Video Tape Log

Disk File Name

PER_15.XLS

Using This Form

Rather than labeling and relabeling tapes over and over again, use this form. Note the contents of a tape in the description section. Then put a small label on the tape spine, using only the number in column A. When you want to view or erase a tape, select it by number. When you rerecord a tape, change the description and reprint the form.

Entering Data

Enter all data directly into unprotected cells on the form. Use values for dates [1] or use the DATE function. To enter tape numbers, enter a number in the first TAPE# box (cell A25) [2] and the other tape numbers will be automatically calculated for you.

Printing This Form

Click the printer tool in the toolbar or choose Print from the File menu.

Adapting This Form

You can use this form to index cassette tapes, photo albums, or even a stamp collection. After unprotecting the worksheet, delete column H (if it's not needed), and enter the title of the new form in cell A21 [3].

Video Tape Log ❸

TAPE #	FORMAT/ DATE	DESCRIPTION	ERASE
1 ❷	VHS 4/91 ❶	Geoffrey's first Christmas 090 to 167. First birthday - 188 to 320	
2	VHS 11/88	MS cooks a perfect Thanksgiving meal -- 00 - 2988 Last episodes St. Elsewhere, Dallas	
3	VHS 12/89	Kids school play -- 0 to 1255	
4	VHS 10/88	State of Union Messages 1989 and 1991	
5	VHS 10/86	Super Bowls: Giants vs Bills / Giants vs Broncos Billy Buckner lets ball go through legs.... @ 4770	Protect
6	VHS		
7	VHS		
8	VHS		
9	8MM		
10	8MM		
11	8MM		
12	8MM		
13	8MM		
14	8MM		
15	8MM		

Running Log

Disk File Name

PER_16.XLS

Using This Form

Use this form to track your running progress. It includes fields for the date, miles run, minutes run, a miles per minute calculation, pulse rate, and comments. This form is best maintained in the worksheet, as the dates are entered automatically and the miles per minute figure is calculated automatically. Nevertheless, like most Winning Forms, the Running Log can also be printed out and filled in on paper.

Entering Data

Begin by entering the month and year in cells B19 and E19 (not shown in the illustration). You can use *This*, *Last*, or *Next* for the month. The form has room for 31 days, and leaves blanks [1] when not all the days are needed. Enter miles [2] and minutes [3] as values to ensure that the miles per minute calculation is performed correctly.

Printing This Form

Click the printer tool in the toolbar or choose Print from the File menu.

Adapting This Form

This form can be easily adapted to track any type of exercise routine, or, more broadly, any type of daily measurements taken over a month, such as weather observations (temperature, barometer, wind speed, precipitation, etc.). To change the form, unprotect the worksheet, then type the new column headings over the old ones, changing column widths as needed.

If you need to delete columns, be careful not to delete the month and year entries, or the date column will cease to function correctly.

(continued)

Running Log

Date	❷ Miles	❸ Minutes	Min/Mile	Pulse	Comments
04/01/93	3.2	23	7.2	95	Light mist, about 65 degrees
04/02/93	2.8	18	6.4	102	Mid-course Windsprints; 70 deg, clear
04/03/93					
04/04/93					
04/05/93					
04/06/93					
04/07/93					
04/08/93					
04/09/93					
04/10/93					
04/11/93					
04/12/93					
04/13/93					
04/14/93					
04/15/93					
04/16/93					
04/17/93					
04/18/93					
04/19/93					
04/20/93					
04/21/93					
04/22/93					
04/23/93					
04/24/93					
04/25/93					
04/26/93					
04/27/93					
04/28/93					
04/29/93					
04/30/93					
❶					

Running Log (continued)

Formula Notes

The date column is based on a table below and to the right of the body of the form. These formulas determine the number of days in the month, and translate the entries typed on row 19 (such as *Sep* or *Next*) into something Excel understands.

CHAPTER

7

SALES AND MARKETING

Selling a product or service is the beginning of business success. The sales and marketing forms in this section will help you to focus on the important tasks of forecasting and tracking your sales activities.

The section also contains forms for analyzing advertising and direct mail, recording sales, and tracking receipts, prospects, and customers.

Product-Line Sales Projections

Disk File Name

SAL_01.XLS

Using This Form

This form tracks the forecast and actual sales of products in a product line, and calculates variances. The form lists this month's figures, the year-to-date figures, and the estimated year-end figures. It can be used either on paper or electronically.

Entering Data

Enter all data into unprotected cells. First type the date into the space provided [1], then type the product descriptions in the leftmost column [2]. You may then enter forecast [3] and actual [4] data for the current month, the year to date, and the estimated year-end. Variances are calculated automatically.

Printing This Form

Click the printer tool in the toolbar or choose Print from the File menu.

Adapting This Form

This form can be used in any context that demands forecast versus actual figures for the current month, year to date, and estimated year-end, along with calculated variances. You can also track individual products instead of product lines. To extend the form to additional products or product lines (beyond 15), simply insert additional rows.

If you decide to insert additional rows, remember to reset the heights of the new rows, for consistency. It is best to avoid inserting at the top of ranges, as the total formulas will not automatically adjust to include the new data. After you have inserted the new row, use the Edit Copy command to copy the formats and formulas from existing rows.

Product Line Sales Projections

October 1993 ❶

❷

Product Line	MONTH ❸			YEAR TO DATE			ESTIMATED YEAR END		
	Forecast	❹ Actual	Variance	Forecast	Actual	Variance	Forecast	Actual	Variance
Dry Goods	$24,000	$21,870	($2,130)	$237,000	$231,543	($5,457)	$310,000	$300,000	($10,000)
Yard Goods	18,000	17,145	(855)	157,500	162,304	4,804	205,000	210,000	5,000
Confections	6,800	9,480	2,680	76,500	82,130	5,630	100,000	107,000	7,000
Hardware	37,500	42,066	4,566	423,000	456,205	33,205	550,000	585,000	35,000
Totals	$86,300	$90,561	$4,261	$894,000	$932,182	$38,182	$1,165,000	$1,202,000	$37,000

Product Sales Goals

Disk File Name

SAL_02.XLS

Using This Form

Use this form to help set and analyze the monthly sales goals of up to
three products or product lines. Last year's monthly sales are com-
pared to this year's monthly goals, and a change is calculated. This
form is best filled out in the worksheet.

Entering Data

Begin by entering the date and by specifying whether the analysis is
in dollars or units [1]. Next, enter the names of the products or lines
[2] you'll be analyzing. Enter the remaining data into the unprotected cells. The totals and change are calculated automatically.

Printing This Form

Click the printer tool in the toolbar or choose Print from the File
menu.

Adapting This Form

In addition to product sales, this form can be used to track any three
divisions, departments, or territories. Similarly, it can track expenses,
cost savings, and other financial measures. The form can basically be
used for any three items that are tracked monthly, had a last-year figure, and for which goals are set this year.

Formula Notes

The months in column A are determined by analyzing the first
month with a lookup table below and to the right of the form. Note
that the formulas are not case-sensitive; that is, it makes no difference whether you type in upper- or lowercase. It is also interesting to
note that only the first three letters of the month are relevant to the
formula. For instance, January and Jane have the same effect, as do
March and Mary, July and Julie.

Product Sales Goals

1993 Units ❶

	ROCK		❷	PAPER			SCISSORS			TOTAL		
	Last Yr	Goal	Change	Last Yr	Goal	Change	Last Yr	Goal	Change	Last Yr	Goal	Change
Jan	1,782	2,000	12%	325	350	8%	711	800	13%	2,818	3,150	12%
Feb	1,523	1,700	12%	158	200	27%	564	650	15%	2,245	2,550	14%
Mar	1,901	2,000	5%	168	200	19%	740	850	15%	2,809	3,050	9%
Apr	2,308	2,400	4%	365	400	10%	642	700	9%	3,315	3,500	6%
May	2,538	2,800	10%	402	450	12%	663	800	21%	3,603	4,050	12%
Jun	1,866	2,000	7%	217	250	15%	604	700	16%	2,687	2,950	10%
Jul	2,212	2,500	13%	264	300	14%	653	800	23%	3,129	3,600	15%
Aug	1,998	2,300	15%	267	300	12%	537	600	12%	2,802	3,200	14%
Sep	2,054	2,000	-3%	318	350	10%	741	900	21%	3,113	3,250	4%
Oct	2,117	2,400	13%	159	200	26%	554	650	17%	2,830	3,250	15%
Nov	1,430	1,600	12%	193	200	4%	657	800	22%	2,280	2,600	14%
Dec	1,859	2,100	13%	426	450	6%	732	850	16%	3,017	3,400	13%
Year	23,588	25,800	9%	3,262	3,650	12%	7,798	9,100	17%	34,648	38,550	11%

Prepared by: _____ Dick Schnary and Ed Settera

Date: 01/12/93

Sales Tracking Worksheet

Disk File Name

SAL_03.XLS

Using This Form

This form is used to track, by customer, one month of both new sales and reorders of products. It compares actual sales to the goal for the month, and calculates the variance. This form is intended to be used electronically.

Entering Data

Enter all data into unprotected cells. Enter the date in cell J24 [1]. Variances and totals are calculated automatically.

Printing This Form

Click the printer tool in the toolbar or choose Print from the File menu.

Adapting This Form

This form can be applied to any situation in which it makes sense to track new business and reorders on a monthly basis.

Sales Tracking Worksheet

For January, 1993

Prepared by   Ike N. Dewitt

Date   February 3, 1993 ❶

Company and Product	New Business			Reorders			Total		
	Goal	Actual	Variance	Goal	Actual	Variance	Goal	Actual	Variance
Star Federated: Dry Goods	$18	$12	($6)	$48	$54	$6	$66	$66	$0
Yard Goods	12	8	(4)	32	25	(7)	44	33	(11)
Confections	24	26	2	36	41	5	60	67	7
Hardware	34	24	(10)	0	0	0	34	24	(10)
United Drug: Dry Goods	7	8	1	32	35	3	39	43	4
Confections	17	29	12	192	221	29	209	250	41
HARCO: Hardware	38	32	(6)	201	185	(16)	239	217	(22)
Total	$150	$139	($11)	$541	$561	$20	$691	$700	$9

Monthly Sales Projections

Disk File Name

SAL_04.XLS

Using This Form

Use this form to track one year of sales projections for a salesperson or department. The form tracks both new business and reorders, and can be used either on paper or electronically.

Entering Data

Enter sales goals and actual sales into unprotected cells. Variances and totals are calculated automatically. You can change the starting month by typing the first three letters of the month name in cell A32 [1].

Printing This Form

Click the printer tool in the toolbar or choose Print from the File menu.

Adapting This Form

This form can be applied to any situation in which it makes sense to track new business and reorders on a yearly basis. If your business does not track sales in this manner, you can change the titles to type of sale (for example, Direct [2] and Channel [3]).

Formula Notes

The months in column A are determined by analyzing the first month with a lookup table below and to the right of the form. Note that the formulas are not case-sensitive; that is, it makes no difference whether you type in upper- or lowercase. It is also interesting to note that only the first three letters of the month are relevant to the formula. For instance, January and Jane have the same effect, as do March and Mary, July and Julie.

Monthly Sales Projections
(In Units)

Salesperson or Department Lois S. DeMette   Date   2 April 1993

	NEW BUSINESS ❷			REORDERS ❸			TOTAL		
	Goal	Actual	Variance	Goal	Actual	Variance	Goal	Actual	Variance
❶ Jan	5	1	-4	40	43	3	45	44	-1
Feb	7	8	1	60	64	4	67	72	5
Mar	8	10	2	70	76	6	78	86	8
Apr	10	14	4	80	93	13	90	107	17
May	12			120			132		
Jun	15			140			155		
Jul	13			110			123		
Aug	11			90			101		
Sep	11			90			101		
Oct	10			80			90		
Nov	8			70			78		
Dec	10			100			110		
Year	120	33	3	1050	276	26	1170	309	29

Prepared by _____

Quarterly Sales Activity Report

Disk File Name

SAL_05.XLS

Using This Form

This form presents four quarters of summary sales statistics, comparing actual versus forecast. Included in the form are sales and profit measures, selling cost, activity, and account information. This form is intended to be filled out in the worksheet.

Entering Data

Enter all data into unprotected cells. Percentages, averages, and totals are calculated automatically.

Printing This Form

Click the printer tool in the toolbar or choose Print from the File menu.

Quarterly Sales Activity Report

Salesperson Amanda Lynn

Territory Great Lakes

Date 12 April 1993

	Q1		Q2		Q3		Q4		Year	
	Forecast	Actual	Forecast	Actual	Forecast	Actual	Forecast	Actual	Forecast	Actual
Gross Sales	247	254	322		220		374		1,163	254
Gross Profit	148	143	174		128		215		665	143
% Gr. Profit to Gr. Sales	59.9%	56.3%	54.0%		58.2%		57.5%		2	1
Net Profit	53	49	64		45		83		245	49
% Net Profit to Gr. Sales	21.5%	19.3%	19.9%		20.5%		22.2%		1	0
Salary	9	9	9		9		9		36	9
Commission	12	11	14		11		15		52	11
Expense: Auto	1	1	1		1		2		5	1
Travel	12	10	14		10		12		48	10
Entertainment	3	2	3		3		3		12	2
Other	2	2	2		2		2		8	2
Total Days Worked	46	45	48		45		47		186	45
Number of Calls Made	160	154	170		150		165		645	154
Average Calls Per Day	3.5	3.4	3.5		3.3		3.5		14	3
Number of New Accounts	3	2	4		2		3		12	2
Number of Accounts Lost	1	0	2		2		1		6	
Number of Accts at Qtr End	135	135	137		137		139		139	135
Number of Potential Accts	50	46	50		50		50		50	46

Prepared by Jim Nastix, Finance and Controls

Direct-Mail Analysis

Disk File Name

SAL_06.XLS

Using This Form

Use this form to run the numbers on a direct-mail campaign. The form includes a breakdown of gross margin of the product being sold, the cost of the direct-mail piece, and an analysis of the profit and break-even point. This form is intended to be used in the worksheet, as it contains many useful formulas. For some mailings, you may know the total cost of each mail unit but not the breakdown of costs for the individual components. In this case, simply enter the total unit cost into the Other [1] field (cell G40), and enter Total Cost into cell F40.

Entering Data

Enter all data into unprotected cells. Enter the date as a value or using the DATE function [2]. Cell G25 uses the mm/dd/yy format.

Printing This Form

Click the printer tool in the toolbar or choose Print from the File menu.

Formula Notes

Cells G58 and G59 [3] enable the user to enter the fixed costs for a mailing. The break-even analysis calculations require these fixed-cost values to return a relevant number. In some cases, you may not know these costs since a supplier might quote you a total job amount for, say, a 50,000-unit mailing inclusive of fixed creative costs. If you wish to determine these break-even calculations, it will be necessary to identify these fixed costs. This will also give you a better understanding of how much it will cost for subsequent mailings of the same piece.

Direct Mail Analysis

Promotion _____ Winning Forms @ 175,000 units _____   Date   **❷** 02/14/92

Gross Margin per Unit	
Selling Price	$50.00
Add: Handling Charge	3.00
Total Revenue per Unit	$53.00
Cost of Merchandise	$16.50
Shipping or Delivery	2.00
Order Processing	0.65
Cost of Returns	1.00
Bad Debt	0.55
Other (Warranty Card)	0.06
Total Cost per Unit	$20.76
Gross Margin per Unit	$32.24

❶

Direct Mail Cost per Unit	
Circulars	$0.15
Letters	0.15
Inserts	0.14
Lift Pieces	0.06
Envelopes	0.10
Order Forms	0.05
List Rental	0.20
Assembly	0.15
Addressing	0.05
Postage	0.14
Other	0.00
Direct Mail Cost per Unit	$1.19

Net Profit and Breakeven Point	
Units Mailed	175,000
Response Rate	4.500%
Unit Sales	7,875
Gross Margin	$253,890
Mailing Costs	$208,250
Fixed Costs	
Creative Development	$12,000
Allocations, Other	500
Total Fixed Costs	$12,500
❸	
Total Net Profit	**$33,140**
Breakeven Unit Sales	2,157
Breakeven Unit Mailing	47,929

Prepared by   Di Meduzzin, Marketing Mgr

Sales Activity Report

Disk File Name

SAL_07.XLS

Using This Form

This form presents summary sales statistics for an individual sales-person, comparing actual versus forecast. Included in the form are sales and profit measures, selling cost, activity, and account information. This form is intended to be filled out in the worksheet.

Entering Data

Enter all data into unprotected cells. Percentages and averages are calculated automatically.

Printing This Form

Click the printer tool in the toolbar or choose Print from the File menu.

Sales Activity Report
For Month Ending 31 March 1993

Salesperson   Amanda Lynn

Territory   Great Lakes   Date   12 April 1993

	FORECAST	ACTUAL
Gross Sales	75.0	77.0
Gross Profit	45.0	46.0
% Gross Profit to Gross Sales	60.0%	59.7%
Net Profit	16.0	15.0
% Net Profit to Gross Sales	21.3%	19.5%
Salary	3.0	3.0
Commission	4.0	3.0
Expense: Auto	0.3	0.3
Travel	3.0	2.5
Entertainment	1.0	0.7
Other	0.7	0.7
Total Days Worked	15.0	15.0
Number of Calls Made	53	49
Average Calls Per Day	3.5	3.3
Number of New Accounts	2	1
Number of Accounts Lost	1	0
Number of Accounts at Period End	135	135
Number of Potential Accounts	50	46

Prepared by   Jim Nastix, Finance and Controls

Media Forecast

Disk File Name

SAL_08.XLS

Using This Form

Use this form to plan your monthly advertising for the next year. Then compare each month's actual expenditures versus the forecast established at the beginning of the year. The form includes categories for radio, magazine, and direct-mail advertising, and more.

Entering Data

Enter all data into unprotected cells. Note that the column headings [1] are unprotected and can be changed by typing over them.

Printing This Form

Click the printer tool in the toolbar or choose Print from the File menu.

Adapting This Form

This versatile form can be used anywhere it makes sense to track monthly actual versus forecast, for up to five items over the course of a year.

Formula Notes

The months in column A are determined by analyzing the first month with a lookup table below and to the right of the form. Note that the formulas are not case-sensitive; that is, it makes no difference whether you type in upper- or lowercase. It is also interesting to note that only the first three letters of the month are relevant to the formula. For instance, January and Jane have the same effect, as do March and Mary, July and Julie.

Media Forecast
For 1993

	Radio Forecast	Radio Actual	Magazine ❶ Forecast	Magazine Actual	Newspaper Forecast	Newspaper Actual	Direct Mail Forecast	Direct Mail Actual	Billboard Forecast	Billboard Actual	Total Forecast	Total Actual
Jan			$5,000	$8,840	$2,870	$4,083			$1,500	$1,258	$9,370	$14,181
Feb			7,000	8,100	2,200	677			1,700	1,852	10,900	10,629
Mar			6,000	9,125	1,390	1,730					7,390	10,855
Apr			10,000	5,900	2,080	3,458					12,080	9,358
May			6,000	7,800	3,070	2,080					9,070	9,880
Jun	6,000	5,490	8,500	6,865	2,720	4,400					17,220	16,755
Jul	7,500		7,000		1,360						15,860	
Aug	8,000		8,500		2,060		6,200				24,760	
Sep	7,500		8,500		1,430		7,200				24,630	
Oct			9,500		1,260		7,500				18,260	
Nov			8,000		2,620		6,600		2,100		19,320	
Dec			7,500		2,970				2,400		12,870	
Year	$29,000	$5,490	$91,500	$46,630	$26,030	$16,428	$27,500		$7,700	$3,110	$181,730	$71,658

Date 07/12/93

Prepared by Amanda Reckenwith

Telemarketing Report

Disk File Name

SAL_09.XLS

Using This Form

This form is used to measure the weekly progress of one telemarketing representative. It tracks the number of calls made and the orders placed to both existing and prospective clients. The form can be used either on paper or in the worksheet.

Entering Data

Enter all data into unprotected cells. The week-ending date can be entered either as a value or with the DATE function. Cell J27 uses the mm/dd/yy format [1].

Printing This Form

Click the printer tool in the toolbar or choose Print from the File menu.

Telemarketing Report

Name Morris Bettir_____   Progress for Week of   05/17/93

	Number of Calls Completed				Number of Orders Placed			
	Clients	Goal	Prospects	Goal	Clients	Goal	Prospects	Goal
Monday	14	20	22	25	3	4	2	3
Tuesday	23	25	34	30	4	5	2	4
Wednesday	24	25	38	35	6	5	3	4
Thursday	17	20	41	40	4	4	5	5
Friday	12	15	32	30	5	3	5	4
Saturday	22	20	24	20	2	4	2	3
Total	112	125	191	180	24	25	19	23
Last Week	94	100	163	160	22	21	18	24
% Change	19%	25%	17%	13%	9%	19%	6%	-4%

Notes _____

_____

_____

_____

_____

_____

_____

_____

Monthly Record of Ad Receipts

Disk File Name

SAL_10.XLS

Using This Form

This form tracks one month of orders and receipts from a direct-fulfillment ad in a particular publication. The form contains space for the product, selling price, size and cost of the ad, and so on. The form is intended to be used in the worksheet.

Entering Data

Enter all data into unprotected cells. Enter the month and year in row 19 (not shown in the illustration). To leave the form blank so that the dates can be filled in manually, simply blank out the month and year. Orders and receipts are entered for each day in the month [1]. The running totals [2] are then calculated automatically.

Printing This Form

Click the printer tool in the toolbar or choose Print from the File menu.

Formula Notes

The Total Number of Orders and Total Receipts columns use the MAX function to calculate running totals. For this reason, they do not handle negative numbers in the daily orders or daily receipts. Negative values are treated as though they were zero.

MONTHLY RECORD OF AD RECEIPTS

Product	Selling Price	Key	Month
Safe-T-Lok Washers	$44.99 per case	STL-450	October
Publication	**Circulation**	**Issue**	**On Sale**
SE Plumbers Assn Journal	18,000	October	September 21
Cost	**Size of Ad**	**Monthly Profit**	**Monthly Loss**
$650	1/2 Page		

Day	Daily Number of Orders	Total Number of Orders	Daily Receipts	Total Receipts
10/01/92	5	5	$314.93	$314.93
10/02/92				
10/03/92				
10/04/92	8	13	404.91	719.84
10/05/92	4	17	719.84	1,439.68
10/06/92	11	28	629.86	2,069.54
10/07/92	14	42	854.81	2,924.35
10/08/92	8	50	449.90	3,374.25
10/09/92				
10/10/92				
10/11/92	12	62	629.86	4,004.11
10/12/92	16	78	809.82	4,813.93
10/13/92	17	95	854.81	5,668.74
10/14/92	14	109	719.84	6,388.58
10/15/92	6	115	359.92	6,748.50
10/16/92				
10/17/92				
10/18/92	22	137	1,304.71	8,053.21
10/19/92	18	155	989.78	9,042.99
10/20/92	14	169	764.83	9,807.82
10/21/92	12	181	719.84	10,527.66
10/22/92	19	200	1,124.75	11,652.41
10/23/92				
10/24/92				
10/25/92	13	213	719.84	12,372.25
10/26/92				
10/27/92				
10/28/92				
10/29/92				
10/30/92				
10/31/92				

Telephone Sales Order

Disk File Name

SAL_11.XLS

Using This Form

This form helps you to record telephone sales. When you have completed a sale, send a copy of the form to the customer for confirmation of the order.

Entering Data

Enter dates as values or using the DATE function [1]. Enter the order number as a value or a label [2].

Printing This Form

Click the printer tool in the toolbar or choose Print from the File menu.

fnfn

Telephone Sales Order

WING THINGS
Specializing in Sopwith Camel Parts

Sold To

Hiram Spad
909 Uppena Way
Kitty Hawk NC 88888

Ship To

Same

CUSTOMER NO	HS - 00000
TERMS	On Presentation
SALES	Regular
SHIP WEEK OF	ASAP
SHIP VIA	Mole Tunnel Express
FOB	St. Louis
ROUTING	Circuitous

YOUR ORDER NO.	ORDER DATE	OUR ORDER NO.
TT -PO 0909	6/7/92 ❶	LC - 999 ❷

Interest will be charged at 1.5 % per month.
This equals a rate of 18 % annually.

ITEM	QUANTITY ORDERED	DESCRIPTION	DATE NEEDED	UNIT COUNT	UNIT PRICE	AMOUNT
1	155	Wooden Wing Struts	7/7/92	PIECES	17.35	2689.25
2	222	Canvas	8/1/92	YARDS	8.91	1978.02
3	229	Twisted Wire	ASAP	FEET	9.35	2141.15
4						
5						
6						
					TOTAL	6808.42

Telephone Sales Order Number _____887-998_____

Purchaser's Signature _____ Date _____

Seller's Signature _____ Date _____

Monthly Sales Activity Report

Disk File Name

SAL_12.XLS

Using This Form

This form presents twelve months of summary sales statistics, comparing actual versus forecast. Included in the form are sales and profit measures, selling cost, activity, and account information. This form is intended to be filled out in the worksheet.

Entering Data

Enter all data into unprotected cells. Percentages, averages, and totals are calculated automatically. Change the starting month by typing the first three letters of the month in cell E25 [1]. The other months will be calculated automatically by formulas.

Printing This Form

Click the printer tool in the toolbar or choose Print from the File menu.

Formula Notes

Pay special attention to the summary column at the far right of the form [2]. With most measures, a sum is the appropriate calculation. However, for certain line items (such as profit to sales ratio), summation does not make sense.

Cells Q29, Q31, and Q42 [3] use the same formulas as the rest of the cells in their respective rows, to present an accurate calculation. Cells Q46 and Q47 (Number of Accounts at Month End and Number of Potential Accounts), however, use unusual formulas [4]. In each case, the formula uses the number of entries in the row to index the correct value. Note that this assumes that all entries are contiguous; that is, that there are no blank cells before filled cells.

(continued)

Monthly Sales Activity Report

Salesperson Amanda Lynn   Territory Great Lakes   Date 12 April 1993

	Jan	Feb	Mar	Apr	May	Jun	Jul	Aug	Sep	Oct	Nov	Dec	Year
Gross Sales	91.0	86.0	77.0										254.0
Gross Profit	50.0	47.0	46.0										143.0
% Gross Profit to Gross Sales	54.9%	54.7%	59.7%										56.3%
Net Profit	18.0	16.0	15.0										49.0
% Net Profit to Gross Sales	19.8%	18.6%	19.5%										19.3%
Salary	3.0	3.0	3.0										9.0
Commission	5.0	3.0	3.0										11.0
Expense: Auto	0.3	0.3	0.3										1.0
Travel	4.0	3.5	2.5										10.0
Entertainment	0.9	0.4	0.7										2.0
Other	0.7	0.6	0.7										2.0
Total Days Worked	16.5	13.5	15.0										45.0
Number of Calls Made	58	47	49										154
Average Calls Per Day	3.5	3.5	3.3										3.4
Number of New Accounts	1	0	1										2
Number of Accounts Lost	0	0	0										
Number of Accts at Mth End	133	134	135										135
Number of Potential Accts	45	47	46										46

Prepared by Jim Nastix, Finance and Controls

Monthly Sales Activity Report (continued)

For example, if you enter data for January, February, April, and May (leaving March blank), the year summary column will display the data for April instead of May. There would be four entries, and April is the fourth month. The solution to this problem is to not leave any cells blank. If you don't have data for all months preceding the current month, simply enter NA.

Quotation

Disk File Name

SAL_13.XLS

Using This Form

Use this form to respond to a customer and quote a price for your product or service.

Entering Data

You may enter data on the worksheet or print the form and enter it by hand.

Printing This Form

Click the printer tool in the toolbar or choose Print from the File menu.

FROM:

AUNT BEA'S ATOMIC MUSTARD PLASTERS
1010 Fifth Street
Painesville, OH 08989

QUOTATION

TO:		DATE	**04/18/93**
APOTHECARY PHARMACY AND MED SUPPLIES		F.O.B.	**Sandusky, OH**
101 MOUNTAIN AVENUE		TERMS	**N30 2/10**
SOBERSIDE OR 99999-000		DELIVERY	**PREPAID**
		NUMBER	**09090**

THANK YOU FOR YOUR INQUIRY (2/15/92
WE ARE PLEASED TO QUOTE YOU AS FOLLOWS:

ITEM	QUANTITY	DESCRIPTION	UNIT PRICE	DELIVERY DATE
1	2 GROSS	DELUXE SUPER FAST RELIEVERS - per gross	1.22	IN STOCK
2	3 CASES	COUNTRY LINIMENT AND APC (24 oz., 12 per case	9.60	FEB 23 @ LATEST
3				
4				
5				
6				
7				
8				
9				
10				
11				
12				

We shall be pleased to supply any further information you may
need and trust that you will favor us with an order, which will
receive our prompt and careful attention.

_____   _____
            PER   DATE

Out of Stock Report

Disk File Name

SAL_14.XLS

Using This Form

If you cannot fill an order immediately, use this form to notify the customer of when you can fill it. Print two copies of the form; one for your files and one for the customer. Fold the form at the lines just above the body of the form to display the address box in the window of a standard #9 or #10 envelope. If you can obtain perforated paper from your office supply store, your customer can tear off the bottom of the form and return it to you.

Entering Data

This form contains no formulas, so you can print it as a blank or enter data directly into the form.

Printing This Form

Click the printer tool in the toolbar or choose Print from the File menu.

JELLY JARS, INC.

101 ADFAF ROAD
PUNGENT SPRINGS, AK 09090
(909) 787-7878
FAX# (909) 999 - 1212

To:

Annie's Vermont Condiments
897 Secaucus Road
MOONACHIE, NJ 07777

DATE	04/22/93
YOUR ORDER NO	8899-009
YOUR ORDER DATE	04/18/93
OUR ORDER NO	AD-8899

OUT OF STOCK REPORT

#	ITEM NO	DESCRIPTION	QTY	EST SHIP
1	PJ-0011	Embossed Pint Jars with glass caps	125	04/25/93
2				
3				
4				
5				
6				
7				
8				
9				
10				

WE ARE TEMPORARILY OUT OF STOCK ON THE ITEM(S) LISTED ABOVE. PLEASE
COMPLETE THE FORM BELOW AND RETURN IT TO US. WE APOLOGIZE FOR ANY
INCONVENIENCE THIS MAY HAVE CAUSED YOU.

#	SUBSTITUTE [Specify Product #]	BACKORD	CANCEL	PLEASE RETURN THIS FORM TO
1				Ahmin Trubble
2				Jelly Jars, Inc.
3				10101 Old Green Hwy
4				Warm Springs AR
5				90909-9876
6				CUSTOMER
7				Annie's Vermont
8				Condiments
9				CUST ORDER NO:
10				8899-009

Signed _____   Date _____

Sales Prospect Form

Disk File Name

SAL_15.XLS

Using This Form

This form is used to track new sales prospects. It provides space to record details about the prospect, sales activities, planned actions, and an assessment of the prospective customer or client. As there are no formulas in the form, it can be used on paper as well as electronically.

Entering Data

Enter data into the unprotected cells on the form. Note that all entries, including the Approximate Monthly Volume [1], are to be made as labels.

Printing This Form

Click the printer tool in the toolbar or choose Print from the File menu.

Adapting This Form

There are no formulas in this form; therefore, it can be very easily modified to your specific needs. For example, you may wish to add your company logo to the top of the form. An even more basic enhancement would involve entering the territory name or even the sales rep's name.

SALES PROSPECT FORM

New ☐   Update ☒ Follow-up Date ___February 13, 1993_____

Company Name Rockway Sanitation, Inc._____

Contact ___Bill Jawatta_____ Title ___Procurement Manager____

Address ___1 Rockway Square_____

___Roquefort, OR 97501_____

Phone ___(503) 555-1212_____

Market Segment Industrial Sanitation_____

Call-in ☐   Referral ☒   Referred by ___Len DeHand_____

Current Supplier don't know_____

❶ Approximate Monthly Volume $32,000_____

Form Letters Sent   "New Year's Resolution" intro letter_____

Material Sent Brochure, Small Sample Kit_____

Sales Calls (date and summary) _____

_____

_____

_____

_____

Date and Summary of Last Discussion_____

_____

_____

_____

Desirability as Client Very High ☐   High ☒   Medium ☐   Low ☐

Probability of Closing   100% ☐   75% ☐   50% ☒   25% ☐

General Comments _____

_____

_____

_____

_____

Commission Report

Disk File Name

SAL_16.XLS

Using This Form

Use one form for each salesperson to record sales, commission rates, and commissions payable. The form can be used either on paper or electronically, though the automatic commission calculations will save you time.

Entering Data

Enter all data into unprotected cells. Dates can be entered either as values or with the DATE function [1].

Printing This Form

Click the printer tool in the toolbar or choose Print from the File menu.

Formula Notes

Note that the formulas in the Amount column round the commission earned to two decimal places. Though this assures that what you see on the spreadsheet is what is calculated by the total formula, you may wish to operate at a lesser (or greater) level of precision. For example, to change the formula to whole dollars, simply change the ROUND function to use zero instead of two decimals.

Commission Report

Name: May K. Living

From: 01-Mar-93 ❶
To: 15-Mar-93

Order Date	Order Number	Account	Invoice Amt	Commission Rate	Amount
02-Mar	JB03-7323	COMMCO	$2,369.57	5.75%	$136.25
05-Mar	IA72-9021	JCBURO	9,984.62	3.50%	349.46
06-Mar	IE82-4356	ABMAB	1,290.43	7.50%	96.78
10-Mar	JC43-6734	ETWENS	5,579.35	5.75%	320.81
12-Mar	JG98-1241	COMMCO	8,439.50	5.75%	485.27
12-Mar	KC67-5903	ABMAB	12,894.00	3.50%	451.29

Total Sales | $40,557.47

Total Commission Earned | $1,839.86
Less Advance | 800.00
Commission Payable | $1,039.86

23-Mar-93

_____
SIGNED

DATE

Customer Ledger

Disk File Name

SAL_17.XLS

Using This Form

Use this form to record all orders placed by a given customer. After you have created a form for each customer, you will have the beginnings of a customer order data base.

Entering Data

This form contains no calculations. You may enter data by hand or directly into the worksheet. Dates [1] are entered as values.

Printing This Form

Click the printer tool in the toolbar or choose Print from the File menu.

Adapting This Form

There are no formulas in this form; therefore, it can be very easily modified to your specific needs. For example, you may wish to add your company logo to the top of the form.

Design Notes

Separating every five rows of data by the double lines and the shaded numbers [2] is a technique you can use in your own forms.

The Flimber Company

CUSTOMER LEDGER

NAME | Annie's Vermont Condiments
ADDRESS 876 Secaucus Industrial Park
CITY Moonachie   STATE MA
ZIP | 02022-09091

CUSTOMER PHONE | 201-999-0909
CUSTOMER FAX | 201-555-9999
PURCHASING MGR | Lydia Coffan

	PURCHASE ORDER #	SALES ORDER #	DATE	ACCT #	QTY	DESCRIPTION	PART #	VIA	SHIPPED	BILLED
1	JJ-0099	CCH0099	6/12/92	OA000	600	Happy Face Jelly Jars	JR-999	P.I.E.	6/15/92	6/22/92
2										
3										
4										
5										
6										
7										
8										
9										
10										
11										
12										
13										
14										
15										
16										
17										
18										
19										
20										
21										
22										
23										
24										
25										

(The DATE column header spans SHIPPED and BILLED.)

INDEX